Toddler Sleep Training

The Ultimate Guide to Getting Your Children to Fall Asleep Fast and Sleep Through the Night

© Copyright 2020

The content contained within this book may not be reproduced, duplicated or transmitted without direct written permission from the author or the publisher.

Under no circumstances will any blame or legal responsibility be held against the publisher, or author, for any damages, reparation, or monetary loss due to the information contained within this book, either directly or indirectly.

Legal Notice:

This book is copyright protected. It is only for personal use. You cannot amend, distribute, sell, use, quote or paraphrase any part, or the content within this book, without the consent of the author or publisher.

Disclaimer Notice:

Please note the information contained within this document is for educational and entertainment purposes only. All effort has been executed to present accurate, up to date, reliable, complete information. No warranties of any kind are declared or implied. Readers acknowledge that the author is not engaging in the rendering of legal, financial, medical or professional advice. The content within this book has been derived from various sources. Please consult a licensed professional before attempting any techniques outlined in this book.

By reading this document, the reader agrees that under no circumstances is the author responsible for any losses, direct or indirect, that are incurred as a result of the use of information contained within this document, including, but not limited to, errors, omissions, or inaccuracies.

Contents

INTRODUCTION 1

CHAPTER 1: THE NON-SLEEPY TODDLER: A CAUSE FOR
CONCERN? 3
    Sleep Regression and What to Expect When It Happens 4
    Signs that Your Toddler is Sleep Deprived 7
    When Should You Seek Medical Advice? 8

CHAPTER 2: UNDERSTANDING TODDLER SLEEP 10
    How Much Sleep Does Your Baby/Toddler/Child Need? 11
    Stages of Sleep 14
    Factors that Disrupt a Toddler's Sleep 17
    Other Potential Effects 21

CHAPTER 3: SLEEP ASSOCIATIONS 23
    Negative Sleep Associations 24
    Positive Sleep Associations Defined and How to Introduce
    Them 30

CHAPTER 4: NIGHT FEEDING 33
    When Should You Stop Night Feeding? 34
    Effective Tips to Stop Night Feeding 35
    Is it Necessary to Wean your Toddler from Night Feeding? 39

CHAPTER 5: THE CO-SLEEPING TODDLER: TO ENCOURAGE OR
PROHIBIT? 41
    The Proven Benefits of Co-sleeping 43

Do's and Don'ts for Safe Co-Sleeping 46
CHAPTER 6: MANAGING NIGHTTIME FEARS 53
  Stages of Sleep and How They Relate to Nighttime Fears 55
  Causes of Nighttime Fears 55
  How to Deal with Nighttime Fears in Toddlers 56
  When Should You Contact a Doctor? 60
CHAPTER 7: NIGHTMARES AND BEDWETTING 63
  Nightmares in Toddlers Defined 63
  What Makes Nightmares Different from Night Terrors? 64
  Common Causes of Nightmares in Toddlers 65
  Dealing with Nightmares in Toddlers 67
  How to Avoid Bedwetting 71
CHAPTER 8: SLEEPWALKING AND SLEEP TALKING 73
  What Should You Know About Sleepwalking in Kids? 74
  How to Deal with Sleepwalking in Toddlers and Kids 76
  When to Seek Medical Help 79
  What Do You Need to Know About Sleep Talking? 81
  What Can You Do About Sleep Talking? 82
CHAPTER 9: SETTING A SLEEP SCHEDULE 84
  When Should You Start Setting Up a Sleep Schedule? 85
  What is the Ideal Sleep Schedule for Toddlers? 85
  Effective Tips for Setting Up a Sleep Schedule for Toddlers 86
  Mistakes to Avoid When Setting a Sleep Schedule for your
  Toddler 90
CHAPTER 10: THE GROWING TODDLER: DEALING WITH CHANGE 94
  Making Adjustments on Various Sleeping Routines and Habits 95
  One- to Two-year-old Routines 96
  Transitioning to a New and Big Bed 97
  Dealing with Sudden Changes in a Preschooler's Sleep
  |Schedule 101
CONCLUSION 104
HERE'S ANOTHER BOOK BY MERYL KAUFMAN THAT YOU MIGHT LIKE 105

Introduction

Do you have a toddler whose sleeping habits continue to wear you out? If you answered "Yes" to that question, please know that you are not alone. Many parents have experienced the same problem and are aware of how exhausting and challenging it can be. In fact, it is one of the most challenging experiences that most parents have to handle, whether they are first-time parents or not.

Friends and family may have tried consoling you by telling you that this experience will pass. However, when exactly will that happen? Even if your toddler slept well when they were still an infant, toddlerhood might be a challenge since they will most likely be at a stage when their energy is at an all-time high. With that said, expect sleep to be the last thing they will want to do when it's bedtime.

Fortunately, there are ways to train your toddler to sleep, and this book will serve as your guide to help you apply those methods. This toddler sleep-training book is different from others you may have read. It contains useful tips and techniques that your child is likely to respond positively to as well.

Most of the sleep-training tips you will learn are up to date, so they will certainly work in these modern times. They are easy to follow and understand, so you can start using them immediately to train your toddler(s) to have happy dreams through the night. This book also uses tips specifically designed for toddlers and kids, so expect positive responses quickly.

Chapter 1: The Non-Sleepy Toddler: A Cause for Concern?

A familiar scenario among parents, whether they are first-timers or not, is having a smooth-sailing parenting experience once their babies overcome their sleeping difficulties and adapt better nighttime habits. The trouble is, they then end up being haunted by yet another challenge that affects their baby's sleep upon reaching toddlerhood.

Do you have the same problem? If so, it could be because of sleep regression, which often happens once babies are two years old, but sometimes as early as eighteen months. Your experience may be good overall before that stage. While it is true you may still have experienced instances when your child did not sleep well—because of teething or a medical issue—their sleeping habits were still good most nights.

Now that your toddler has reached the age when sleep regression often kicks in, things become more challenging and difficult for you. You will likely be exhausted from tending to their needs every time they decide they do not want to sleep.

Aside from the fatigue and its possible effects on your mood and overall health, many parents worry about their toddler's health and welfare. You may be worried about whether their inability to sleep will take a toll on their wellbeing. So, what really happens if your toddler cannot go to sleep? Should their sleep regression be a cause for concern? Is it time to visit their pediatrician or other medical specialists? Time to find out.

Sleep Regression and What to Expect When It Happens

Sleep regression is a scenario that occurs when your baby or toddler, who has had good sleeping patterns in the past, begins to wake up—often at night (in worse cases, they wakes up every twenty minutes) or displays behaviors that may have a negative impact on their sleep. These include taking shorter naps than usual or skipping them altogether for no clear reason. This regression may occur for a specific period—around three to six weeks in most cases.

If you are already used to putting your toddler to sleep without difficulty, this new scenario may take you off guard. You will most likely feel frustrated, not knowing what to do and how you can make them complete the required number of hours of sleep they need every day.

Your frustration will probably grow when you notice their inadequate sleep affecting several aspects of their growth and development. The sleep deprivation of both parents and toddler can also make your parenting tasks more difficult to fulfill. Aside from that, you may notice your toddler exhibiting temper tantrums and defiant and oppositional behavior. Why? The answer is because it is the natural result of sleep deprivation.

Imagine those scenarios if you have not experienced them yet, and you will most likely cringe at the thought of having to deal with such issues any time soon. Your child's defiant behavior may add to the fatigue and exhaustion you may have already felt. The even bigger problem is that both elements—their newfound sleeplessness and defiance—may likewise begin to influence each other.

You will notice them starting to refuse your requests, refuse taking naps, or stubbornly shouting or crying incessantly every time their sleep is disrupted at night. The insufficient sleep brought on by your toddler's sleep regression can also cause them to become crankier, eventually resulting in temper tantrums. Be aware that all the symptoms will reveal themselves and you will notice.

Those are just a few of the common scenarios that might happen when your toddler cannot get enough sleep. One way to combat those unwanted instances is to learn as much as you can about sleep regression. It would be best to familiarize yourself with the specific stages in your child's life when this is most likely to happen.

Knowing when to expect it, you can prepare yourself and set up techniques that will help you both handle the situation. Also, keep in mind that each baby or toddler is different. This means that your toddler's sleep regression signs may differ from the behaviors of others.

Though, in most cases, babies or toddlers undergo sleep regression during the following ages:

- **Four months** – The four-month sleep regression is indeed one of the most difficult stages in a parent's life. Most parents dread this specific stage as it is usually the first time their child's sleeping patterns are disrupted.

If your baby deals with sleep regression at this age, remember there are logical reasons for it. The most common reasons why your baby starts to show sleep problems are hunger caused by a growth spurt, the pain brought on by teething, and the fun and excitement they may feel as they learn to roll over.

- **Six months** – Sleep regression may also happen during your baby's sixth month. It is mainly because of the growth spurt they will most likely experience during this time, but take note: This is also the time when babies are already capable of sleeping through the night.

Most of them will just wake up for simple cuddles. As far as that is concerned, it would be best if you test a certain technique to train them to sleep well during this stage so that you will have a lower chance of dealing with the negative effects of sleep regression in the future. Small adjustments make all the difference, so try different techniques to make your baby feel secure.

- **Eight months** – This could go on until your child is up to ten months old. Note that this is the specific period when your baby will start to crawl. At around ten months, they may also start to stand up on their own. These new skills might disrupt their sleeping patterns. It would also be normal for babies to deal with separation anxiety during this stage. It might lead to them waking up at night, as they will seek your reassurance.

- **12 months** – Sleep regression during this age may be brought on by the new skills that your baby has started to acquire. It could be as simple as learning to stand up or taking their first steps. These huge milestones might disrupt their usual sleeping patterns, preventing them from going through the night.

Also, many toddlers undergo sleep regression upon reaching around eighteen to twenty-four months old because of certain factors like night terrors, nightmares, separation anxiety, teething, and fear of the dark.

Apart from familiarizing yourself with the specific ages or stages when sleep regression usually occurs, it is also advisable to determine the specific signs that indicate sleep deprivation. This is not just for your toddler, but also for what you as their caregiver may experience. That way, you can immediately take action if anyone shows severe signs of sleep deprivation that should be a cause for concern.

Signs that Your Toddler is Sleep Deprived

So, how do you know if your toddler is already sleep deprived and starting to display symptoms of health issues and other unwanted behaviors? Here are the usual signs you need to watch out for:

- Clinginess and constant tantrums
- The tendency to reject drinks and foods
- Crying more often than usual
- Complete meltdowns in public places, like in grocery stores
- Problems with concentration
- Being hard to wake up in the morning
- Tending to sleep spontaneously during the day or take naps unintentionally
- Irritability and moodiness
- Prone to getting frustrated easily
- Crying and getting angry easily

Certain fluctuations in your toddler's sleeping patterns are natural during their first few years. Remember that just because your toddler sleeps the entire night upon reaching three to six months does not necessarily mean they will continue to do so for the full duration of their growth and development. Eventually, their patterns may be disturbed, causing them to have a hard time reestablishing a normal and regular sleeping and waking cycle.

When Should You Seek Medical Advice?

You should also know that more severe sleep deprivation symptoms of in toddlers might require a faster and more proactive response, like visiting your doctor. While it is true that your toddler's inadequate sleep brought on by sleep regression tends to go away naturally after a while, it is still advisable to contact your doctor if they display more alarming symptoms.

Do not also hesitate to visit a doctor if you have any questions about your baby's sleep or want to discuss identified causes of their sleep problems, such as persistent nightmares. Aside from those, the following warrants a doctor's visit or consultation:

- **When your toddler has breathing difficulties** – They may produce noise when breathing, stop breathing for a while when asleep, or snore. Those signs usually indicate sleep apnea. One thing to take note of is that babies below six months often experience irregular breathing.

They also most likely pause in between breaths for around five to ten seconds. However, if your toddler tends to breathe or snore loudly, wake up choking and gagging, or pause their breath for at least twenty seconds, do not hesitate to seek your doctor's advice as it might be sleep apnea, which requires immediate treatment.

- **When you notice that your toddler displays unusual nighttime behaviors** – These include having an unexpectedly high number of nighttime awakenings or fears that only become apparent at night. You also need your toddler's pediatrician's or doctor's advice if their sleep problems start to affect their daytime behaviors.

- **When they display signs of gastroesophageal reflux** – One of these signs is frequent spitting or vomiting of substantial amounts of consumed milk. They may also tend to wake up screaming due to pain. This condition usually occurs when the valve connecting the esophagus and stomach does not function properly.

When the valve malfunctions, it can force the acidic contents of your toddler's stomach back up into their esophagus and mouth. It can be a serious condition that requires medical treatment, so be observant of your toddler's symptoms.

- **When they cannot seem to sleep because of an illness** - If their inability to sleep is caused by pain or fever due to an underlying illness or condition, like an ear infection, teething, or upset stomach, contacting your doctor may be the most viable option for you and will certainly help you to feel more confident.

Just make sure you are also fully knowledgeable of the illness's specific signs or symptoms that warrant a call to your pediatrician. The more serious signs are a fever over 101.5 degrees Fahrenheit (if the child is at least six months old), an earache, swollen glands, and bloody nasal discharge.

You may also consider visiting your baby's pediatrician if you have already applied a specific sleep training technique for over two weeks without seeing any improvements in their sleep. If you do this consistently only to notice your baby is still disturbed during sleep without any apparent reason, their doctor or pediatrician might be able to provide insight or advice on improving the child's sleep.

Also, remember that while true sleep regression and deprivation is not the most fun part of parenting and there is a chance that certain signs and symptoms may require a doctor's help, it is still normal in the majority of cases. If your toddler does not show signs of a major illness that cause them to be unable to sleep, do not worry too much. This stage will most likely pass. Just give it enough time.

Moreover, do not forget to continue sticking to normal sleep and bedtime routines. Make sure these routines are reassuring for your little one. Soon enough, they will get used to sleeping soundly again.

Chapter 2: Understanding Toddler Sleep

A vital aspect of your child's development is sufficient and proper sleep, so you have to make sure that you understand it completely. One thing you have to take note of in this area is that while infants tend to have plenty of sleep, toddlers usually display this strange ability to resist it, especially during times when they need it.

As a parent, it should be your goal to crack the sleep deprivation code of your toddler. That way, you can help them achieve their much-needed restorative rest. If you do not change their unwanted sleeping habits, they are at risk of depriving themselves of the specific amount of rest and sleep they need.

This could lead to them developing behavioral and learning problems, depression, and emotional instability. Inadequate sleep may also make them prone to becoming obese or suffering from other health issues.

How Much Sleep Does Your Baby/Toddler/Child Need?

The first thing you should crack is the specific number of hours of sleep your baby or toddler needs every day, and that will depend on their age. Here is a rough estimate of their sleeping requirements, as well as information about the sleep patterns and habits of babies and toddlers during certain stages.

0 - 3 Months (Newborns)

Newborns, including babies around zero to three months, usually sleep around the clock. In most cases, they sleep for around ten to eighteen hours daily, though their schedules are often irregular. They will likely be awake for around one to three hours daily.

The sleep-wake cycle of infants or newborns also usually depends on their need for feeding, nurturing, and changing clothes or diapers. One vital point to note is that the total hours of sleep required by newborns do not need to be continuous. This means that the period of their sleep can last for several minutes to hours.

Even when asleep, expect the baby to be still active. They may twitch their legs and arms, suck, smile, or generally look restless. If you have a newborn, note that they can show their need for sleep in various ways. Among the signs indicating this is fussing, crying incessantly, and constant rubbing of the eyes.

It would be best for you to put your newborn to bed every time they feel sleepy, instead of when they are already asleep. This move will increase their likelihood of sleeping quickly and training themselves to sleep. You can also encourage your baby to have less sleep during the daytime by keeping them exposed to noise and light and increasing playtime.

You should then turn their environment into a dimmer and quieter one and lessen their activity during the evening. That way, you encourage them to sleep more at night. You are reinforcing the sleeping/waking cycle by doing this.

4 - 11 Months (Infants)

During this age, infants need around nine to twelve hours of sleep at night and around half an hour to two hours of naps during the day, which can be spread out over one to four times. Also, take note that when your baby reaches six months, it is unnecessary to give them nighttime feedings.

This is because they can already sleep through the night. However, only around 70 to 80 percent of babies or infants can master the habit of sleeping through the night once they hit nine months. You may want to start training yourself to put your infant to bed when they are still drowsy rather than fully asleep.

This technique will turn them into a self-soother, allowing them to sleep independently during bedtime and go back to sleep on their own whenever they wake up at night. As much as possible, do not allow them to get used to the habit of looking for parental assistance every time they go to bed.

Infants accustomed to using this behavior are prone to becoming signalers and crying incessantly at night as they need their parents' help every time their sleep is disrupted. Moreover, remember that your infant's developmental and social issues can influence their sleep during this stage.

You will notice that secure infants attached to their caregivers display only minimal sleep issues, but these same infants may also hesitate to give up such kinds of attachment for sleep. Because of that, expect them to deal with separation anxiety that might disrupt their sleep patterns, mostly in the second half of their first year. Other possible disruptions during this stage are increased motor development and any illness.

1 - 2 Years (Toddlers)

If your little one has already reached toddlerhood, the number of hours of sleep they need daily is around eleven to fourteen hours. At around eighteen months, their naptimes' frequency will most likely go down to just once daily, lasting for around one to three hours. You should avoid scheduling their naps close to their bedtime schedule, though, as doing so may only prevent them from sleeping on time at night.

Also, toddlers are at the age when they are more prone to showing plenty of sleep issues, like extreme resistance to going to bed and frequent nighttime awakenings. It is also common for them to have nightmares and nighttime fears. Several factors can cause such problems.

Among them is the strong drive to become more independent and increase social, cognitive, and motor skills. All these tend to interfere with their normal sleeping patterns.

Aside from that, factors like separation anxiety, desire to have independence, and development of their imagination can also trigger sleep issues. To determine if your toddler is already experiencing such problems, watch to see if they start displaying behavioral problems and daytime sleepiness.

3 - 5 Years (Preschoolers)

Preschoolers, around three to five years old, need eleven to thirteen hours of sleep every night. They also usually have short naps, around thirty minutes to an hour or two. Just like toddlers, a preschooler may also have a hard time falling asleep at night. They may also find it difficult to wake up in the morning.

The fact that their imagination is already further developed may also cause them to have nightmares and nighttime fears. The preschool stage is also when sleep terrors and sleepwalking are often at their peak.

6 - 13 Years (School-Aged Children)

When your child becomes school age, around six to thirteen years old, the number of hours they need to sleep daily will be reduced to nine to eleven hours. It is also when more and more distractions can affect their sleep. Among them are certain TV shows and the Internet, media, and computers. These things might cause not only sleeping difficulties but also nightmares.

Besides that, watching TV shows close to their bedtime schedule may also lead to sleep resistance, fewer sleeping hours, and anxiety during bedtime. Moreover, there are things that your child may need to prioritize once they reach the school-age years. These include school and social activities, sports, and other recreational activities that take up a huge chunk of their time. Such demands may also affect their sleep.

Stages of Sleep

Just like adults, toddlers and children also have different stages of sleep. You have to learn about these stages if you want to deal with any sleep-related difficulties your child may be experiencing. Before learning about such stages, though, it is important to remind yourself that sleep is vital, as it is the brain's main activity during your child's early development.

The sleep-wake cycle, or what is referred to as the circadian rhythm, occurs with the darkness and the light regulating it. It also takes time for this rhythm to develop completely, which is why newborns do not have a regular sleep schedule. You can expect such rhythms to start developing at around six weeks.

Upon reaching three to six months, babies will start displaying a more regular sleep and wake cycle. At two, many toddlers have already spent a higher number of hours asleep than awake. This is necessary as sleep is vital for their physical and mental development.

However, as mentioned earlier, certain factors in your child's development might be hampering their ability to sleep and follow normal circadian rhythms. One way to handle this is to be aware of the specific things that happen in your child's sleep—particularly the stages of sleep.

- **Stage 1** - Often characterized by drowsiness, the first stage of sleep is what your baby goes through. Here, they begin to fall asleep, but not deeply.
- **Stage 2** - This stage, also called active or REM (rapid eye movement) sleep, is characterized by your little one twitching or jerking their arms or legs. You may also notice their eyes moving beneath their closed eyelids. It is considered the active stage since your baby tends to participate in the whole process. Their brain is still active, which is also the reason why dreaming happens during this stage.

This stage may also be a time when your baby's breathing becomes irregular. It even tends to stop for around five to ten seconds, which may be due to a condition referred to as infancy's normal periodic breathing. Note that these pauses will not cause the color of your baby's skin to change. After the pause, expect rapid breathing to recommence.

It usually comes at 50 to 60 breaths per minute for around ten to fifteen seconds. After that, their regular breathing pattern returns until the whole cycle is repeated. Most babies usually outgrow this periodic breathing cycle upon reaching six months or so.

- **Stage 3** - After the active or REM sleep, the third stage comes, characterized by light sleep. Here, you will notice your baby displaying more regular breathing patterns and rates. Their sleep will also be less active.

- **Stage 4** - The deep non-REM sleep is the next stage in your baby's sleeping cycle. It is also called quiet sleep. Here, your child is in a much deeper sleep, so expect active movements like twitching to stop. You will notice your baby falling into a progressively deeper sleep. Once they are at this stage, it will be harder to wake them up.

It is crucial to reach this stage, as it is the most vital aspect of sleep. It is the time when your child's body performs its most important functions. This depth of sleep that your child experiences causes: an increased supply of blood to their muscles, significant restoration of their energy, and the stimulation of tissue growth and repair.

This is when their body releases vital hormones necessary for proper healthy growth and development.

In most cases, babies tend to dedicate half of their time to every stage or state. The sleep cycle also tends to be completed in around 50 minutes. Upon reaching six months, thirty percent of your baby's sleep consists of the REM stage. During their preschool age, expect the entire sleep cycle to take place every 90 minutes.

You also have to realize that the sleep cycle does not necessarily progress using the mentioned stages in sequence. You can expect sleep to start at the first stage and progress to the second and third stages. After the third stage, though, there is a great possibility for your child to go back to the second stage before they get to REM sleep.

Once the REM sleep is completed, the body will return to the second stage. It is possible for your child's sleep to cycle through the four stages around four to five times the entire night. Another thing to note is that while many people think of sleep as a passive and inactive process, it has been discovered that the human brain remains active during its various stages.

It is the reason why the body still functions, even when one is asleep. With that, sleep contributes much toward performing a wide range of processes, including cleansing the brain and consolidating memories.

Factors that Disrupt a Toddler's Sleep

This book has lightly touched on the possible disruptions to a toddler's or child's sleep when it comes to the required number of hours of sleep based on age. To understand these disruptions even better and act on them appropriately, they are categorized as follows:

Sleep Changes/Shifts

At around three to six months, many babies may need to make many adjustments to their sleeping patterns. This change or shift in sleep is usually characterized by the need to be awake more during the daytime and sleep longer at night. It is also when the toddler's sleeping cycle begins to resemble that of an adult—alternating between light and deep sleep.

The problem is that if your toddler gets into this stage, they are at risk of being unable to handle the change, causing disruptions to their normal cycle. It may happen whenever they shift between each stage of sleep. This shift may cause them to wake up and be unable to put themselves back to sleep.

Note that this scenario also occurs in older kids and adults. They also tend to wake up at night for such reasons; however, they already know how to put themselves back to sleep right away. Since toddlers and children have not yet mastered this skill, they may lose precious hours of sleep.

Certain Breakthroughs or Milestones

Sleep disruptions in toddlers also often come in the form of breakthroughs and milestones. Note that a lot of parents frequently report sleep deprivation and regression in kids upon learning new skills, like crawling, rolling over, and standing. In this case, your toddler may be overwhelmed with the new skill they have learned.

It might occupy their mind too much, increasing their desire to practice and hone the skill always, even during bedtime. Moreover, if they have just acquired the skill of standing up on their own, there is a great possibility that they will do it all the time in their crib. Your toddler may stand up when they wake up in the middle of the night and may struggle to go back to sleep because they cannot put themselves back down.

Environmental Changes

Another category that may interrupt your toddler's sleep is a change of environment. Note that even minor changes in surroundings can have a major impact on their sleep. Even if they slept well in the past, a sudden change in the weather, for instance, can significantly affect room temperature.

It might lead to discomfort at night, making them unable to sleep. Another possible reason is the new outdoor lighting that penetrates their room. If this is still new to them, it might keep them up.

Separation Anxiety

Your toddler's sleep may also be interrupted by separation anxiety. At six to twelve months, a baby may start to understand whenever they are away from you. If neither parent is in their room, it may cause them to get anxious. The peak of this problem often happens at ten to eighteen months, though it fades once they hit two.

However, you will notice your toddler waking up more than usual at night because of this separation anxiety. They may end up crying, looking for you, or trying to get out of their crib. Your toddler may also have a strong urge to sleep beside you. While separation anxiety is very challenging, remember that it is normal. It is a part of their emotional development, so you should not worry too much about it.

Sudden Changes in Routines

If you suddenly change routines, this may negatively affect your child's normal sleeping patterns. It could occur when traveling together, causing them to stay up late, which they are not used to. It could also occur when they suddenly fall ill, causing them to get used to either parent checking up on them every night.

They may get used to the feeling of being soothed or rocked to sleep because of the illness, so they may want you to do the same even after they have recovered. Note that every time regular routines change, their sleep patterns may be temporarily thrown out of balance.

Possible Effects of Lack of Sleep in Toddlers and Children

Aside from learning about the stages of sleep and the number of hours that your child needs for sleep depending on their age, it is also crucial to gather as much information as possible about the effects of lack of sleep in toddlers and children. That way, you will have an idea of what actually happens if your child lacks sleep or does not sleep the whole night.

By learning these possible effects, you will be more motivated to find ways to correct their sleeping patterns and train them to be a good sleeper.

Poor Cognitive Abilities

If you do not do something to correct your child's sleeping problems, they will most likely be deprived of much-needed sleep, which is essential to boost their cognitive abilities. Keep in mind that sleep is the main nutrition needed by the brain. It plays a major role in the growth and development of their cognitive function.

Adequate sleep is also vital for your baby's body to accomplish its intended functions, especially during the first few months and years of life. Those who sleep well have a better chance of establishing stronger brain architecture than those who do not. The problem is that those who suffer from insufficient sleep may also lose their chance to develop vital cognitive skills as they grow.

Moreover, sleep contributes a lot to raising smart kids. Parents must train their kids to sleep without any interruptions if they want them to grow into faster and better learners. It is because of the importance of sleep in their cognitive function.

With well-developed cognitive skills, your toddler can also display better language skills, focus, and attention spans. With that, expect them to digest and absorb new information with ease. Aside from that, adequate sleep is also vital for creativity. If they do not get enough sleep, their cognitive function will most likely suffer, leading to lower rates of learning and cognitive development.

Delayed Growth

It is also highly likely that your child's growth and development will suffer from a lack of sleep. Sufficient sleep plays a major role in ensuring that they grow properly and at the right pace. Also, toddlers and kids tend to grow daily when they are sleeping properly.

It is the time when the brain releases growth hormones into the bloodstream. If they are deprived of sleep, it might limit the production and release of such growth hormones, leading to a significant delay in your toddler's growth and development.

Prone to Obesity

If your child does not sleep well at night, their body's metabolic development may also be drastically affected, making them prone to becoming overweight. Most toddlers and kids deprived of the right amount of sleep tend to gain excess weight, though at a slower pace. It can lead to an energy imbalance that can further increase their risk of becoming overweight.

Also, take note that sufficient sleep is needed to maintain a healthy hormonal balance. If your toddler does not get sufficient sleep, it might lead to a hormonal imbalance that further triggers constant hunger. Left uncontrolled, they will be at risk of becoming obese.

Aside from that, poor and insufficient sleep can also be linked to increased insulin secretion. Insulin plays a vital role in the control and regulation of glucose processing. It also contributes to promoting the storage of fats. If your child's insulin level gets too high, they will most likely gain weight unnecessarily. It might even make them prone to having to deal with diabetes. Therefore, having too little sleep can raise your child's insulin levels, thereby boosting their chances of becoming overweight.

Poor Memory

If your child has insufficient sleep, it is also possible that they may suffer from a poor ability to retain memories and information. As a result, they may have learning difficulties. Note that the brain plays a vital function of collecting and storing memories created throughout the entire day into a part of the brain that deals with memory retention and habits. It does so to organize such memories, making it possible to retrieve them in the future.

The human brain does such a vital function during the REM stage. It usually happens when toddlers and kids dream. If your toddler does not get the amount of sleep they need every day, there is a high chance that this vital function will be blocked. It can harm their immediate memory.

Other Potential Effects

A toddler is also at risk of displaying the following effects if their poor sleeping habits, including insufficient sleep, are not corrected right away:

- Weakened immune system
- A sudden increase in appetite
- Defiant behaviors
- Overly emotional behaviors: It could be having no patience or very little patience, extreme sensitivity, easily hurt feelings, and explosive temper tantrums
- Medical conditions that may appear in the future

Again, it is worth reiterating that sleep regressions are normal, but if you notice that your child already displays major side effects from their inability to meet their required sleep, taking action is essential. This is even more important if their sleep regression goes over the expected level at this age, around two to six weeks.

You have to start training them to sleep well. You can begin with the sleep training methods that are discussed in the remaining chapters of this book. Before applying any technique or method, though, consider consulting a doctor or pediatrician so that you can better decide what method works appropriately for your toddler.

Chapter 3: Sleep Associations

The first technique a parent can use to teach toddlers and children to sleep well is sleep associations. If you are unfamiliar with it, note that it refers to anything your child or toddler associates with sleep and falling asleep. Common examples of sleep associations in toddlers are their favorite stuffed animals, a blanket, or a pacifier.

Sleep associations encompass not only objects but actions, too—ones that you or their caregiver often do to make them fall asleep. These include nursing and rocking them to sleep or co-sleeping—letting them sleep next to you or their caregiver. Note that kids begin to create these associations early in life.

For instance, if you make your toddler sleep by feeding them with a bottle of milk or rocking them to sleep, they will look for this same routine every time it is bedtime. It would be like reinforcing to them that they cannot sleep if you do not feed them. This habit is good during their first few months, but you need to break this sleep association as they get older as it can be unhealthy. It might promote cavities or become a source of unnecessary and extra calories.

With that in mind, it is safe to say that while there are positive associations, there are also negative effects on a toddler. It is the reason why training your toddler to settle and sleep on their own requires addressing negative sleep associations that they are already used to. It is advisable to get rid of the negative associations and introduce positive ones. That way, your toddler can master the art of soothing themselves without looking for that unnecessary action they have to become familiar with.

Negative Sleep Associations

Negative sleep associations refer to those things that your toddler cannot recreate on their own. This means that if they completely depend on it to get to sleep, they will most likely need your help all the time to find it in case they wake up in the middle of the night.

While these negative sleep associations are fine during your baby's first few months, you must start sleep training as soon as they hit around four to six months by slowly eliminating these things. If you do not, those will also haunt you in the long run as those are the major causes of night-waking and their inability to sleep again without help.

By not correcting this habit, they will most likely continue with this night-waking pattern, negatively affecting both the parent and caregiver and the toddler themselves. Here are just a few of the most common negative sleep associations you should slowly break off if you want to train your toddler to sleep well with no disruptions or interruptions:

• **Pacifier** – Several newborns depend on a pacifier to comfort them. The problem is that sometimes parents take too long to wean their toddlers off using pacifiers. Eventually, the pacifier will turn into a sleep crutch for toddlers and children.

If you let your toddler sleep while sucking on their pacifier and letting it fall out naturally once they fall into a deep sleep, they will look for it whenever they wake up, making it hard for them to go back to sleep. You cannot expect them to sleep again comfortably without it.

- **Rocking to sleep** – If your toddler is used to falling asleep only when you rock them, they will always need you to do it for them whenever they wake. Your toddler will constantly look for you. If you do not break this habit, they will always need your help to sleep.

- **Feeding** – Some toddlers strongly associate feeding with sleeping. It has already been tackled earlier that feeding your child to sleep is not always a good idea, especially long term. You must wean them off this habit as they grow older; otherwise, they will end up always looking for a bottle of milk whenever they wake up, so they can put themselves back to sleep, even if it is unnecessary.

- **Motion Sleep** – This sleep association usually results from putting your baby in the carrier, car, or stroller to make them fall asleep during their first few months. Doing this is not that bad if your baby is still under four months. At such an age, letting them sleep through motion will not have a negative impact, but it will no longer be restorative if you still do it when your baby is over four months. It might even cause their sleep debt to pile up.

- **Co-sleeping** – If your toddler cannot seem to sleep without you in the room, it will eventually cause problems. Besides affecting your toddler's sleep, the need to be around for them to fall asleep will also prevent you from having your much-needed rest.

Note that any sleep association that adversely impacts your toddler's sleep, your sleep, their caregiver's sleep, and other family members' sleep can be considered negative.

If you do not get rid of these things soon, those same things that helped your child sleep in the past will stop them from doing so through the night in the future. Because they have not yet mastered the art of settling themselves to sleep, the problem is that they will then stay awake unless you help them.

How to Correct and Fix Negative Sleep Associations

Once you have identified the specific negative sleep associations preventing your child and yourself or their caregiver from getting much-needed sleep, you must find ways to break these habits. While fixing these issues might be challenging, you can still handle them by applying the right tips. By resolving their negative sleep associations, you and your child will be able to enjoy complete rest.

Just make sure that before starting the fix, everyone at home, including caregivers, is aware of what will happen. Inform them about the need to improve your toddler's sleeping habits. By doing that, no one will give in whenever your toddler looks for the items they need to get to sleep.

Also, make sure you are firm in changing the perception of who is fully in control at home. Do not make the mistake of giving in to your child's persistent misbehaviors and tantrums, as it may only ruin their progress during training. True, it is extremely hard to control toddlers' behavior, especially because they still do not understand right and wrong.

As a parent, you should be responsible for setting and maintaining firm boundaries and guidelines regarding sleeping routines and bedtime schedules. You will only set yourself up for failure during sleep training if you give in and let your child do what they want just because of their stubbornness and loud and incessant crying.

To help you even further when it comes to breaking off negative sleep associations, make a point of following these tips:

Create a Plan that You Can Implement Consistently

Create a plan that you can easily follow through on. It should be something that you and your toddler are comfortable with. That way, you can be consistent in implementing it. For instance, you can create a plan that will cultivate the habit of letting your toddler sleep at a specific bedtime.

Set up more positive bedtime routines that will prepare them for bed. Examples are brushing teeth, a warm bath, and dimming the lights. These routines will signal that it is nearly time for them to sleep. As soon as your child can make minor decisions and choices related to sleep, let them do so too.

For instance, you can let them choose what they want to wear to give them more control over the situation. Giving them some control can encourage them to be ready for bed on time.

Determine the Specific Sleep Association You Intend to Break

Identifying the specific negative sleep association that you intend to eliminate from your child's habits should always form part of toddler sleep training. Note that the best time for you to break it off would be when your baby is around six to twelve months, but you must be very specific and learn as much as you can about negative sleep associations.

It is something that can negatively impact your baby's ability to put themselves to sleep. These include a pacifier, which they can insert into their mouth on their own, a comfort blanket, and white noise. Your goal should be to look for those sleep associations categorized as dysfunctional.

Among these dysfunctional sleep associations are co-sleeping with caregiver or parents, a pacifier that your baby cannot insert into their mouth on their own—requiring you to reinsert it several times every night—and feeding them to sleep. Those are the things that you should focus on removing from your child's habits.

Find Out How You Intend to Remove the Sleep Association

You must decide whether to do it gradually or go cold turkey—which means eliminating it completely and immediately. If you go for the gradual approach, you can slowly get rid of the item they often use to sleep. Just set a certain timeframe when it should be completely removed. Find out which approach—between the gradual and immediate—your child will most likely respond to positively.

Reduce Liquid Intake

Try to reduce the amount of milk or liquid your child gets from the bottle if they associate it with falling asleep again whenever they wake up at night. It is also highly recommended to stretch the specific period in between each feeding throughout the night.

You can substitute this reduction in liquid or milk intake by providing them with more calories throughout the day. Avoid expecting too much, though—even if your baby can sleep for longer than eight hours every night, without feeding or nursing, if they are less than four months old and weigh less than sixteen pounds, they still need feedings.

Remove the Sleep Association Every Time

It would also be best for you to train your child to sleep independently without the sleep association, meaning without you in the room or close by. Just promise them that you will see them when they wake up in the morning.

When doing this tip, you can go for either the modified or unmodified approach. The unmodified approach prevents you from seeing them in their room until the morning. Do make sure that their room is completely safe. Remove anything that might put them in danger.

On the other hand, the modified approach involves checking them regularly, yet you have to do it at an increased time interval. You also have to do it without having to reintroduce the negative sleep association they are used to. Be firm and do not give in, even if your child displays tantrums.

Put Them in the Crib when They're Sleepy

Instead of continuing the habit of putting them into their bed or crib only if they are asleep, do it when they're still awake but already sleepy. This is the approach you have to apply if your child's sleep association involves rocking or swaying to sleep. In case they cry, you can come to their room to offer reassurance using touch and words.

Avoid picking them up, though. Also, stretch the period before you return to their room whenever they cry. Do it slowly, so they can also gradually familiarize themselves with the routine.

Be a More Effective Communicator

In case you notice your toddler feeling bad or crying when you leave them or their own, give them verbal reassurance that you are still around, but they have to stay in their bed so that they can fall asleep. If they get out of bed, take them back without arguing, talking, or making a tremendous fuss.

Keep in mind that it is the tone of your voice that they will hear instead of your words, in most cases. With that said, do not raise your voice or speak at a fast pace. Maintain your reassuring tone and make sure that you do not show any tension in your posture or face.

This will increase your chance of successfully putting them back to bed and leaving the room without them making an enormous deal out of it. It can make them realize that it is indeed time for them to sleep, and you are serious about sticking to that schedule. Be firm when doing this and make sure you continue to communicate with them effectively.

Introduce Positive Sleep Associations

Remember that sleep associations are not entirely negative. This is because some can produce positive results. You have to do introduce these positive sleep associations to your toddler so that they will take advantage of them instead of the negative ones. Learn about these positive sleep associations in the next section of this chapter.

Positive Sleep Associations Defined and How to Introduce Them

Positive sleep associations are among the most favorable elements that you can use for successful toddler sleep training. As the name suggests, these things are all positive, meaning they can make your toddler feel good about the thought of sleeping. Aside from being favorable for your toddler, these things are also good for you.

These associations are positive and will help to guide your baby to sleep the entire night independently. When they do that, you or their caregiver will also gain much-needed rest. Introducing positive sleep associations is crucial if you are already working on the stage of breaking off negative sleep associations, like having to hold, feed, or rock your child to sleep.

To help introduce positive sleep associations and replace negative ones, you must know examples of them. Among those positive associations that can get your child involved are the following:

- Rubbing, biting, or holding a comfort blanket or lovey
- Singing and humming
- Sucking on their fingers or thumb
- Rocking back and forth on their own
- Banging their feet against their mattress
- Lifting their legs to get them into a fetal position

Make sure that you introduce those that your child can do independently, so they can train themselves to get settled to sleep without your help or the aid of their caregiver. You may also want to introduce positive external sleep associations.

These refer to those things capable of setting the scene or environment for sleep. They also refer to all those positive cues telling the child it is already bedtime. The external sleep associations your toddler can use are:

- White noise
- Blackout shades
- A room temperature between 68 to 72 degrees
- A lovey designed to comfort toddlers and kids and make them soothe themselves

It is advisable to slowly introduce positive sleep associations while also starting to break off the negative ones. For instance, you may want to introduce a sleeping bag to comfort the child if they are used to getting fed for them to fall asleep. Feed them to sleep while you zip them into their sleeping bag.

Tuck a small blanket between you and them while you are feeding them from a bottle. This can make them associate the blanket and the sleeping bag with you and the cozy feeling brought on by it with sleep. Eventually, you can put them down while they are still drowsy and not fully asleep.

Also, soon enough, you can finally put them to bed awake and fully settled while they cuddle with this blanket and snuggle on their sleeping bag. You can do this slowly until you no longer need to be around to make them fall asleep.

You can find other healthy and positive sleep associations and habits you can introduce to your child. Just make sure you pick those that are suitable for them and your family's needs and meet the recommendations of a pediatrician.

Another way to develop positive sleep associations is to build out-of-the-nursery sleeping and bedtime routines. This means you can still rock, cuddle, and feed your child but out of the nursery or their room. You also have to do all these things when your toddler is still awake. By doing that, they will not associate sleeping with them having to sit with you or their caregiver in the rocker before you finally put them in their crib.

Moreover, one thing you have to remember about introducing positive sleep associations is that they are intended to help your toddler learn the basics of self-soothing. That way, they can naturally create positive sleep associations and use them whenever they wake up at night. This means you no longer have to get involved in putting them back to sleep.

Just make sure that you completely get rid of negative sleep associations so they can create new and positive ones on their own. Another thing to remember with using this technique to train your baby to sleep is to practice consistency. You must be consistent while training them, so they can finally sleep the entire night independently.

Chapter 4: Night Feeding

One of the sleep associations discussed earlier is feeding your baby to sleep at bedtime. However, take note that some babies and toddlers also get used to the habit of not only feeding at bedtime but also whenever they wake up in the night when they want to experience the same thing because they associate it with going to sleep.

This means they cannot fall asleep again unless you offer them a bottle of milk or your breast. This is called night feeding, which is elaborated on later in this chapter. One key thing to take note of is that night feeding is actually good for babies. It can help them fall asleep or go back to sleep quickly at night, but it will no longer be a good idea once they get older.

Aside from the risk of disrupted sleep affecting both of you, they are also at risk of taking in more calories and feeding more than is necessary. This is because there are times when your baby looks for a bottle or your breast in the middle of the night for comfort rather than hunger.

If you think it is already time for you to wean your toddler off the night feeding, make sure you are truly prepared for it. Arm yourself with information about how you can do it successfully and expect resistance.

When Should You Stop Night Feeding?

Before you wean your child from milk bottles, make sure they are truly ready for it. The following are signs that it is indeed time for you to stop feeding them at night:

- **They are growing well** – Observe your toddler's growth and development. If you notice they are growing well, maybe it is safe for you to stop the night feeding. If you notice their growth is not yet enough, delay the weaning a bit as they will still need the additional calories from night feeding to grow.

- **They are at least six months old** – Another thing you have to consider is the age of your child. Note that infants fed with a bottle can already be weaned off night feeding as soon as they reach six months. If you are breastfeeding, it may take longer. You may even have to wait for at least a year to wean.

- **They tend to wake up inconsistently** – You will also know it is time to wean your child from the night bottles if they tend to wake up at different times during the night. It is a sign their sleep disruptions are not truly brought on by hunger, making night feeding unnecessary. There are also instances when they wake up because they want comfort and help to fall back to sleep.

- **They have less of an appetite during the day** – If you notice your toddler eating less during the daytime, and waking at night to have a feed, maybe it is time to start weaning. It could be that they are asking to be fed at night out of habit.

- **They have dietary changes** – Some babies who have been introduced to solid foods tend to stop feeding at night on their own. If your baby is not one of them, the time when you introduce solid foods to them should also be when you should start gradually weaning them off night bottles. You need to stop night feeding as they already receive additional calories from solid foods.

One thing you should know, though: Even if they display any of the symptoms above, every baby is unique. It means that each night-weaning adventure is also different. If you want to wean them from night feeding, you should remind yourself it is not a good idea to do it during a time when major transitions occur, like when you are switching or moving jobs.

It is not also advisable to make changes to your baby's habit that will significantly affect their sleeping schedule if they are suffering from an illness or dealing with a growth spurt. Moreover, avoid doing the weaning if you will be on a family vacation or during holidays.

Note that no matter how gentle and gradual your chosen night weaning approach is, you still have to do it at the right time—one that will not cause your baby to deal with one stress after another. Try to wait for the right moment. It should be that time when you and your baby are calm, and they seem to be fully prepared for the huge change.

Effective Tips to Stop Night Feeding

If the timing is right and you think your toddler can already handle the weaning, you should be ready to apply those tips that will work for them. Also, constantly remind yourself that you need to listen to the needs of your baby. If a specific tip or technique does not work at first, go onto something else. Do try it again in the future, though.

To make the night weaning more manageable, here are a few tips you can apply:

- **Water down the milk** – This tip is gentle but highly effective in weaning your baby off the bottles at night. What you should do is to dilute their milk slowly using water. Do this for a few nights.

For instance, on the first night, you can offer them a bottle with 75 percent milk and twenty-five percent water. Gradually reduce the percentage of milk over the next few days until each bottle is 100 percent water.

In most cases, offering pure water for a couple of days can make them realize that they do not have to be fed milk to fall asleep. With that, you will notice them starting to resettle themselves and master the habit of sleeping through on their own.

- **Address their hunger clock** - It is one of the first steps you have to undertake when trying to stop your child from feeding at night to make them sleep more peacefully. You can do this tip by ensuring they get most of the calories they need daily during the daytime.

It, therefore, means you have to avoid waiting until nighttime for them to feast. To make this tip work, have a record of everything that forms part of their daily diet. Once you have a log or record of their daily diet, consult your doctor, especially if you are not yet sure about how you can meet your child's daily nutritional needs.

Also, make sure that they are not extremely tired every time you put them to bed at night. By making sure they get proper rest—and enough of it—they will be able to accept certain changes in their diet, as well as correct their hunger clock much easier. You also have to be consistent, so you can successfully integrate the new habits into their system.

- **Go cold turkey** - Many consider this tip as the quickest technique when it comes to weaning babies and toddlers off the bottle. However, be fully prepared if you intend to follow this approach as it requires a strong commitment.

Also, make sure you are tough enough to implement this approach since you will most likely encounter many late-night protests and tears from your toddler. This is because this technique involves the immediate and complete removal of the night feeding.

It might be necessary for you to substitute the milk feeding with other effective strategies for sleep training, like a gradual retreat and controlled cycling. These alternative strategies can help your child develop the important skill of self-soothing, allowing them to go back to sleep without the bottle.

When you plan to go cold turkey, be strongly committed to the entire process. Never give them your breast, a bottle, or a feed. But be observant when implementing this approach. If you notice them become sick all of a sudden, it would be much better to stop doing it for a while and continue when they recover.

- **Gradually reduce the amount of milk they drink at night** – You can expect this tip to work whether you feed your baby using formula milk or breast milk. What you have to do to make this tip work is lessen the volume you offer to your baby or toddler. It could involve less milk in the bottle or decreased time of breastfeeding.

When using this technique, it is also highly recommended to do another sleep training strategy, so your child will immediately get your message that the milk offered is the only drink available. Knowing that, they can also start to practice the art of self-settling whenever they need to return to sleep.

Moreover, make it a point to make a reduction or change gradually. If you are breastfeeding, be ready to deal with a lot more challenges since your baby will most likely have negative responses. They may respond by pulling, grabbing, and protesting whenever you take them off your breast.

With that in mind, never start this tip if you do not have a solid sleep training strategy that will surely work along with the decreased feeding. You should further try to curb your toddler's habit of falling asleep with a bottle or your breast.

- **Nurse more during the day** – Another way to wean your baby from night feeding is to increase the frequency and volume of nursing or bottle-feeding during the daytime. For instance, you may prefer to give them milk every two hours or so instead of the usual three to four hours.

By doing that, they can consume more milk throughout the day, which will most likely lead to a lower chance of asking for milk at night or waking at night just to feed. Also, make sure there are no distractions whenever you feed or nurse them during the day. They will also start to associate drinking as a daytime activity rather than assuming they should do it at night.

Do the nursing or feeding in a room without any distractions. The room should be dim and should have closed doors. If you have other older kids, get them busy, so they will not disturb you and the baby whenever you nurse or feed. Moreover, try to nurse when you are lying down.

Note that babies and toddlers tend to get easily distracted when you feed them during the daytime, causing them to consume less milk than necessary. The problem with that is it might lead to them making up for insufficient milk consumption by feeding more frequently at night. If they do that, you have to be serious about eliminating distractions during daytime feeding so you can maximize it for both them and you.

- **Introduce a cup early** – If possible, introduce your baby to a cup before they turn one or two. Note that it might be harder to stop your child from night feeding as they get older since there is a high chance they will get emotionally attached to your breast or their bottle.

They may associate it with sleep, contributing to the development of the habit of searching for the breast or bottle whenever they wake up if you have decided to use a cup, bottle feed, or nurse at scheduled times. Set a schedule for using the cup too. You may want to use the cup during daytime hours together with solids.

- **Try dream feeding** – This means waking or half-waking them to have an extra feeding at night. The goal here is to make sure their stomach is full enough, so they have a lower chance of waking up and looking for milk in the middle of the night.

You should do this extra feeding before your bedtime, so they will be full enough until both of you are well rested. Another way to do it is to wait for them to wake up and give them a feeding, provided it has been over four hours since the time you last fed them. Do not give them another feeding until they get up in the morning.

One more thing to be aware of is that babies' and toddlers' internal timetables—as far as sleeping through the night is concerned—greatly differ. With that in mind, you can see parents being more comfortable with the thought of allowing their babies or toddlers to lead in terms of night weaning. However, other parents and toddlers tend to deal with a significant decline in the quality of their lives because of night nursing and feeding.

With that said, observe your own situation and your baby. If you notice the night feeding or nursing does not seem to work for both of you, start making changes. Integrate new habits and changes into your usual routines while still considering your child's needs.

You should have the primary goal of maximizing the quality of sleep for everyone. Keep track of your progress so you will know if the night weaning techniques you have implemented work. If such is the case, you can pat yourself on the back for that major achievement. If it does not seem to work, do not give up, as there are still plenty of available strategies. You just have to figure out which one works for you and your baby.

Is it Necessary to Wean your Toddler from Night Feeding?

As a parent, you may have many concerns about stopping your child from feeding at night, especially if they are already used to it. But if you notice it is already affecting their supposed-to-be peaceful sleep and yours, or the sleep of your family, it is necessary to start weaning your child from this habit.

To start training them to resettle without feeding, you have to decide it is indeed necessary for them to let go of the habit. Also, make sure everyone involved in taking care of them commits to trying their best to help them resettle at night by stopping night feeding.

Do not give in to the urge to give them a bottle just to stop them from crying, as it may only lead to confusion. It might also result in you having to spend more time than usual to wean them from the bottle. Your goal is to train them to sleep without the need to rely too much on bottles or feeds.

Another point to remember is that your decision to wean your child ensures they will not get too many unnecessary calories from milk at night. Apart from that, you can expect them to start eating more during the daytime. This is a good thing if you want to train them to eat healthier, solid foods and supply their body with all the nutrition they need by correcting poor eating habits.

The good news is that by deciding to take bottles and feeds away at night, you will notice a quick and significant improvement in the quality of their sleep. Just be consistent and get everyone on board when it comes to implementing the plan, and you will see your toddler quickly adapting to the new habit and sleeping soundly through the night.

Chapter 5: The Co-sleeping Toddler: To Encourage or Prohibit?

Co-sleeping is a popular sleeping arrangement for new parents, especially those who have just gone home with their new bundle of joy. This sleeping arrangement usually involves sleeping in the same area as your baby sleeps. It does not necessarily mean sleeping in the same bed.

As long as you are close to your child and are in the same room, it is already called co-sleeping. It is more on sensory proximity than physical proximity. In other words, you are co-sleeping if you are in one exact spot where you can smell, touch, hear, or see them without any obstacle.

It is a broad concept that covers various sleeping arrangements, including the following:

• *Bed-sharing* – This involves letting your baby sleep with you and/or your partner every day.

- *Sidecar arrangement* – This is the secure attachment of a crib to one side of the bed, usually on the mom's side. All the other sides of the crib stay intact, except for the one next to the parent. This specific side is taken out or lowered so the baby and mother can easily access each other. If you plan to have this sleeping arrangement, take note that you can use a commercial co-sleeper or a sidecar crib, which attaches easily to a bed.

- *Multiple beds but set up in a similar room* – These could include a crib or bassinet set up close to the parents, usually within just an arm's reach. This arrangement may also include a bed or pallet for your older child set up at the foot of your bed or the floor next to your bed.

- *Welcoming your child into your bed whenever necessary* – Using this arrangement, you have already set aside a bedroom for your baby, but you are willing to welcome them into your bedroom anytime. Many families practice this, letting their kids begin their sleeping hours in their separate bedrooms but allowing them to get inside their parents' room when they wake up at night.

While co-sleeping is generally beneficial and practiced in many cultures in different parts of the world, keep in mind that there has also been a mix of opinions about this practice, as it has a few risks. Also, note that while other cultures perceive co-sleeping as a natural solution for letting parents have enough rest while bonding with their babies, a few also focus more on privacy and independence and do not agree with the practice.

Still, many parents are fully aware of the many good things that co-sleeping can offer. It is more beneficial during the first few months of your baby's life. As soon as they get older, it would be best to let them transition to sleeping in their own area or room because co-sleeping may no longer be as beneficial for your child when they get older. If you do not do the transition at the right time, they may end up having problems with their overall quality of sleep.

The Proven Benefits of Co-sleeping

As mentioned earlier, co-sleeping carries several benefits during the early stages of the child's life. It is for this reason that this practice is encouraged in many cultures and families. The following are just a few of the advantages that you and your baby can get from deciding to co-sleep:

Promotes Long and Sound Sleep for You and Your Baby

One major advantage of co-sleeping is that it allows your baby to sleep longer and more soundly. It is mainly because your baby will be more at ease when they feel like you are just next to them. Aside from that, letting them sleep beside you also means that you get to respond to their needs right away. It further gives them a sense of safety and security.

It also promotes better sleep for you, as you no longer need to get up, turn on the lights, and walk to their room whenever they cry or suddenly wake up at night. Whatever is causing them to wake up, you can address it at once. With that, both of you can return to sleep easily and without too much fuss.

Promotes Successful Breastfeeding

By putting your baby close to you, you have a higher chance of becoming successful as a breastfeeding mom. Many moms agree that the key solution for successful breastfeeding at night is co-sleeping. Co-sleeping and breastfeeding even go hand-in-hand since babies who sleep together with their moms tend to breastfeed more often than those who sleep independently or separately.

It will also be less stressful for you since you do not need to get up anytime at night and visit their room to nurse. The only thing that you must do if you are co-sleeping is to help them latch properly, so both of you can go back to sleep. Through co-sleeping, you can nurse without having to wake up completely. Thus, it will be much easier for you to enjoy a complete sleep cycle and get enough rest.

Moreover, your position when sleeping together with your baby seems much safer for them than when you surround them with smothering pillows and harmful blankets. Just make sure that you create a nightly routine that you and your baby can follow so both can enjoy a restful and uninterrupted sleep.

Offers a Great Bonding Experience

Co-sleeping also seems to work well for a lot of parents, particularly those who cannot seem to give their entire time during the day to their babies because of work and other personal matters. If you are a working mom, you are at risk of not spending a huge part of your time caring for your baby.

In that case, the only period when you can bond and spend quality time with them is at night, which is why co-sleeping is much better for you. If you put them in another room, you will be deprived of the chance to enjoy precious bonding moments with them. Co-sleeping is a much better arrangement if that is the case, as it will strengthen and reinforce your closeness.

You can cuddle and do things that they will surely love, like singing them to sleep or reading a bedtime story. Those are just minor rituals and activities, but they are often enough to promote an excellent bonding experience and make your baby feel safe and secure with your touch.

Increases Your Awareness

Co-sleeping also promotes better awareness about all their movements, and you will be more aware of their movements subconsciously. Such awareness is a huge advantage that you will instantly notice if your baby shows movements that are no longer normal, such as having a high temperature or experiencing breathing pauses.

You will also become more aware of your baby's needs. For instance, you will know right away if you need to change their diaper or cover them up with a blanket. Moreover, you can immediately respond to anything that makes them uncomfortable before it disrupts their sleep. The fact that they are close to you is also a huge advantage in case of emergencies.

Are there Disadvantages to Co-sleeping?

While co-sleeping presents numerous advantages to both the baby and parents, it is still vital to learn about a few disadvantages. That way, you can better decide if this arrangement is one you should be encouraged to do at home or prohibit. The following are a few of the most common disadvantages when it comes to considering co-sleeping:

• *May prolong breastfeeding at night* – Being close to your baby when sleeping at night makes it much easier for them to access your breast for feeding. It is convenient for both of you but can also cause problems in the long run, especially if it causes the feeding to take longer than usual. With prolonged breastfeeding time at night, delays in the specific time when your baby falls asleep may occur.

• *Potential safety issues* – This is because your baby may be at risk of being suffocated or crushed when you share the bed. Aside from that, this arrangement also tends to increase the risk of SIDS, which stands for sudden infant death syndrome.

SIDS refers to a baby's sudden death because of suffocation. It affects babies below one-year-old due to things like loose sheets and blankets that tend to stop them from breathing. Parents are also considered as risks to their newborns or babies when co-sleeping.

This is because they have the potential to roll over and crush their babies. Moreover, certain habits of parents, such as smoking and drinking, can further raise the risk of SIDS.

- *Can somewhat interfere with your sleep* – If you share a bed with your baby, your sleep may be negatively affected. It could be because having your baby around will make you want to stay alert all the time. This results in you being unable to sleep deeply. Furthermore, sharing the bed or room with your baby may also prevent you from getting intimate with your partner.

- *May become the cause of your baby being completely dependent on you* – Note that sleeping with your baby can negatively affect their development. This is because it might create a strong sense of dependence. If it takes a long time for you to transition them into sleeping on their own, it will be more challenging and harder for the two of you to separate.

This is one of the reasons you should avoid moving them into a separate room or another bed too late in their growing stages, as doing it later than usual can cause them to feel abandoned or rejected. It would be best to transfer them to their own room or sleeping area at around six to eighteen months.

Do's and Don'ts for Safe Co-Sleeping

If you want to make sure that your baby stays safe during co-sleeping, here are a few do's and don'ts to keep in mind:

- Put your baby to sleep on their back. Do not let them sleep on their side or tummy.

- Use an infant or baby swaddle in place of bedding. Make sure that the swaddle is safe for your baby to use. By doing that, you can lower the risk of having your baby's head covered with the blanket unintentionally when they sleep at night.

- Use a firm mattress. It should be moderately hard. Do not use pillows or waterbeds for your baby.

- Ensure there is no space between the bed and the wall to prevent your baby from rolling out and getting trapped.

- Be a responsible parent. This should mean that you have to stop any unsafe and unwanted habits that might put your baby in danger if you co-sleep with them. Never share the bed with your baby if you smoke, take or use sedatives or drugs, or become intoxicated with alcohol.

- Keep track of the room's temperature. This is to prevent overheating.

- Do not let them sleep between you and your spouse/partner. You should position them beside just one parent and away from the bed's edge unless there is a bassinet beside the bed.

- Do not share a room with your baby unless it is completely smoke-free.

- Do not put stuffed animals, soft blankets, and loose pillows close to their face.

Practicing these do's and don'ts will lessen the chance that your baby will experience SIDS.

How Long to Co-sleep?

If you have decided to co-sleep with your baby, you have to set a timeframe for stopping co-sleeping. This is because while it is good for them during the first few months, it can lead to problems over time. It might even affect the quality of their sleep, eventually.

Note that just like when your baby or toddler can wake you up accidentally if you share a room or bed with them, you can also do the same and wake them. Your baby will be at risk of waking up accidentally if you or your partner snore or talk in your sleep.

Your child may also be disturbed by certain movements, like you getting up and going to the bathroom. If you are a breastfeeding mom, you may also disturb their sleep with just the scent of breast milk. It can cause them to wake up too frequently.

With that in mind, you should know exactly when you should stop co-sleeping and train them to sleep independently. As mentioned earlier, it would be ideal to set up a separate space for them to sleep when they are at least six months old.

Some parents say that it would be much safer and more convenient for them to share a room with their babies for up to a year. Remember that situations vary from parent to parent, though, so you have to weigh the unique factors that affect the entire family. This will give you an idea about the length of time you will be co-sleeping.

For instance, it may take longer for you to separate if your child has health issues than when the baby is perfectly healthy. On the other hand, if they are very mobile and a noisy sleeper, it would be much better to train them to sleep in their own space or room sooner than usual.

You may also be more at ease if you put their room next to yours. As a parent, you are fully aware of your own situation. It would also be best for you to trust your instincts in deciding the safest route to take when it comes to co-sleeping.

How to Transition

If you have been co-sleeping with your baby or toddler for quite a while, but you feel it is already time to train them to sleep in another room, you must make sure that the transition is as smooth as possible. Note that if your baby is already used to sharing the bed or room with you, you will find it quite challenging to separate them from you.

To make the transition easier for both of you, here are some effective tips that can help convince your child to sleep in another room and make sure that they can easily adjust to the new environment:

- *Have a casual conversation with your toddler or child about the importance of sleeping on their own* - Before giving them their own room, make sure that you exert an effort to talk with them about what you need to do. Let them know about the benefits of sleeping in their own bed and room.

Does your child talk casually? If you think that your child can already understand what you are talking about, try using positive examples such as other kids they know who can now sleep alone. You must make the talk as positive and encouraging as possible, as this tone can motivate them to do what you are telling them to do.

- *Let your child pick the things they need for self-soothing* - Once you have clearly explained to your toddler what it means to transition to their own bed and room, make sure that you allow them to choose things that will make them more comfortable in their new environment. For instance, allow them to choose a bed as well as bedding.

Give them the freedom to pick the transitional objects designed to help them soothe themselves too. By letting them have the things they are comfortable using, the whole sleep training process will become much easier. It is also a big help in preserving their trust, thereby lowering the risk of them displaying unwanted behaviors, especially during the adjustment period.

- *Do the transition gradually* - This means taking simple and small steps. Note that you do not need to make a huge leap right away since it can also result in your toddler experiencing shock with the sudden change. During the first few days, do not expect them to stay in their bed or room the entire night right away. With that in mind, be willing to do the separation slowly but surely.

For example, during the first night of the transition, sit on their bed after your usual nighttime ritual. Try to stay beside them until they fall asleep. Also, be patient during the first night because even if you are around, there is still a high chance that they will be restless since it is the first time they will be apart from you.

Leave only when they peacefully fall asleep. Once they get used to that, you can still stay with them but move farther away while waiting for them to fall asleep. You can stay at the edge of their bed instead of exactly behind them. If they get used to that again, you can move even further away.

Continue moving further away until the time when they can already fall asleep, even if you are not in the room. The goal here is to take simple and small steps, so they can make the necessary adjustments as you do every change until you get to the final stage, leaving them alone to self-soothe and sleep.

- *Teach your toddler some effective ways to fall asleep alone* – Do not just tell them to stay in bed and sleep. You also have to guide them, so they learn a few techniques that will work for them, as far as letting them fall asleep is concerned. For instance, you can train them to close their eyes while on their bed and focus on having fun and exciting thoughts, like plans for their birthday.

The goal here is to let your child have something fun to think about, so they will be more comfortable sleeping on their own and getting rid of any fears and worries even if you are not beside them.

- *Avoid negative nuances* – You need to make sure that you do not let your child have negative nuances about having their own room. For example, if you are expecting a new baby soon, moving them to another room or bed may cause them to think that the new baby will replace them.

With that in mind, it is best to do the transition in a manner that will not make them feel rejected. One way to do so is to move them to their room around three to six months before or after the new baby comes. That way, the two huge events will not overlap.

- *Find the right approach for your toddler* – Note that different approaches for stopping co-sleeping work, but the one that will be effective for you will be that which suits your family's preferences and the temperament of your baby or toddler.

One approach that may work for you is sitting next to them until they fall asleep because your presence will somewhat reassure them. You may also go for the cold turkey strategy. If you are unsure what approach will work for you, do not hesitate to consult a child development specialist or pediatrician.

With a professional's help, you will surely be guided on finding the proper approach to guarantee success when trying to stop the co-sleeping arrangements.

- *Be consistent* – Once you have chosen a comfortable approach for both you and your baby, make sure to stick with it for a long time. Be consistent when implementing the approach. Note that the entire transition process may take up to three weeks, sometimes longer, but avoid giving up.

Continue implementing your chosen approach, even if your toddler puts up huge protests. Do not give in to the tantrums. Remain firm and consistent without forgetting to reassure them that you will still be there for them, even if they are already in another room.

Provided you take the necessary and correct safety precautions, co-sleeping with your newborn or baby during the early stages of their life is generally safe. Also, deciding to co-sleep or prohibit it at home all depends on you. You are the one who determines what works for you and the entire family since every baby, parent, and circumstance is different.

If you have decided to allow co-sleeping, you must make sure that you are prepared to part with your child as soon as they are ready. Note that it is crucial to teach them independence by letting them settle on their own and sleep.

By successfully transitioning them to the habit of sleeping in their own room, you will be more at ease as you see them significantly improving the quality of their sleep. It is also good for you and everyone who takes care of them because better sleep for your toddler also means that you will finally have the peaceful and deep rest you have been longing for.

Chapter 6: Managing Nighttime Fears

Your toddler's nighttime fears could also be among the major factors affecting the quality of their sleep. These nighttime fears will interrupt the intended deep and peaceful slumber, making it harder to train them to soothe themselves and finally sleep on their own.

Also called sleep or nighttime terrors, these nighttime fears are characterized by episodes of intense fear, flailing, and screaming even while your baby is still asleep. You can see this situation happening together with sleepwalking. Just like sleepwalking, nighttime fears and terrors are among the most undesirable occurrences while your baby or toddler is asleep.

Expect each episode to last from just a few seconds to several minutes, but sometimes episodes will last longer than expected. It is also important to note that night terrors differ from nightmares, though the two seem to be the same. One major difference is that unlike nightmares, you cannot expect toddlers or kids with night terrors to wake up immediately from an episode.

You can see them screaming, kicking, flailing, shouting, sleepwalking, sitting up, and looking terrorized, but they will not wake up completely. You may also have a hard time communicating with a toddler or child who has just experienced an episode of nighttime terror. In most cases, you will find these kids inconsolable.

Another thing to note about night terrors is that while they are usually traumatizing, those who experienced an episode can often sleep normally again right after it. Most of them will not even have any memory about the experience upon waking up in the morning.

However, despite that, this can have a great impact on the quality of your toddler's sleep. Sleep training will become even more challenging because of these nighttime fears and terrors. These episodes are not usually dangerous, just disruptive to sleep patterns.

With that in mind, gather as much information about this scenario as possible, including its causes and potential cures, so you will know exactly how you can still train your toddler to sleep well. You can talk with your pediatrician to ease any anxiety that might have been caused by this nighttime terror.

Inform the doctor if your toddler's nighttime fears frequently cause them to stay up, especially for over thirty minutes. A medical professional is important in this case because it is a big help in ruling out other health problems that might cause the episodes of nighttime fears and terrors.

It is also even more important to seek the help of a doctor in case the night terrors happen more often than usual, causing a significant increase in the level of your toddler's daytime fatigue. It is also important to have a thermometer available to determine whether there has been a change of temperature because sleep terrors are associated with temperature change.

Stages of Sleep and How They Relate to Nighttime Fears

Every time you go to sleep, you will undergo a few stages—four stages, to be exact. The first stage is characterized by light sleep, making it easier for you to wake up anyone in this stage. It is also considered as the early phase of NREM (non-REM sleep). The fact your brain is still active during the first stage is also why waking someone up is easy.

As soon as you reach the second stage, expect your mind to slow down, making it more difficult to wake you up. It can transition you to the third stage, considered the deepest phase of NREM sleep. Upon reaching the third stage, it is impossible to wake you up. The fourth stage, referred to as REM, is a phase through which you can immediately wake up. It is because it's the time when your brain activities are too frequent.

Now the question is: How do all these stages relate to the nighttime fears and terrors your child experiences? The answer is that these episodes usually happen while your toddler transitions from the second to the third stage. Your toddler's nighttime terrors often occur in the third stage, and that is the primary reason you struggle when trying to wake them up.

As the nighttime terrors occur in the third stage—the deepest phase of the entire sleep cycle—it may cause them to struggle to wake up. Moreover, it has been discovered that nighttime fears usually occur because of the fear linked to transitioning from one stage to another.

Causes of Nighttime Fears

Nighttime fears or terrors take place once your toddler gets into the deepest phase of the non-REM sleep. It usually happens between 12:00 a.m. to 2:00 a.m., which indicates how much it affects not only your toddler's sleep but also your sleep and anyone else's who takes care of them. It has several likely causes, including:

- *Excessive tiredness* – Exhausted or tired toddlers are more vulnerable to experiencing night terrors. It is because their exhaustion may trigger more brain activities once they fall asleep.

- *Disruptions on their regular sleeping routines and schedules* – Your toddler or child may also deal with nighttime fears and terrors if the bedtime and sleep schedules they are used to are suddenly changed. If the changes happen for a few days in a row, they will be at risk of experiencing night terrors and confusing events.

- *Genes/heredity* – Another potential cause of nighttime terrors is heredity. It has been discovered that certain tendencies to this problem are likely to be genetic. This means that if any of your family members are dealing with these episodes, it is highly likely your toddler will experience them too.

- *Sleep disorders* – This one is kind of serious and has to be corrected right away. If your child displays symptoms of a sleep disorder, such as restless leg syndrome and sleep apnea, they will also be more prone to having episodes of night terrors.

Apart from the mentioned causes, other factors that might disrupt deep sleep, like anxiety, a full bladder, sudden noise, and excitement, can also trigger an episode or two of night terrors as dealing with illnesses disrupt the sleep patterns.

How to Deal with Nighttime Fears in Toddlers

If your child has nighttime fears and terrors and you are planning to start sleep training them, one of the first few things you have to do is address and counter such fears so that they can sleep peacefully. The good news is that it is not hard to deal with nighttime terrors.

Here are a few simple tips that seem to work in many toddlers and children:

Preventing Night Terrors

If you notice your toddler is experiencing more episodes of night terror than usual, there are a few things you can do to prevent them. For instance, you can break up their sleep. You can do that by noting every detail associated with each episode. For instance, you can record the exact number of minutes between when they fall into a deep sleep and when the night terror happens.

Observe them for a few days and record the time when the night terrors strike. Once you are already familiar with the schedule, wake them up fifteen minutes before you expect an episode of night terror to strike.

Let them stay awake for around five minutes. It would be best to let them move out of the bed during that period. Follow this routine for around one week to find out if it works in stopping the night terrors from happening.

Avoid Touching Them During an Episode

This tip may go against parental instincts because the symptoms of nighttime fears in your child may instantly urge you to go to them and hold them, but stop yourself from doing so as picking them up, rocking them, hugging them tightly, or doing anything to touch and calm them down will only worsen things.

Many parents even report that the episode becomes shorter whenever they let it end on its own rather than touching their kids. In your case, you can try lying next to your toddler or child instead while ensuring you are not touching them. It allows you to comfort them and make them feel safe and secure without having to touch them.

Introduce a Bedtime Routine

Before doing so, determine the specific number of hours of sleep your child needs. Note that how much they need to sleep will depend on their age. For instance, babies around four to twelve months often need twelve to sixteen hours daily, including naps. If you have a toddler around one to two years old, your goal is to let them sleep eleven to fourteen hours daily.

You can lessen the number of nighttime terror episodes by ensuring your toddler gets the right amount of sleep. You can achieve that by introducing a bedtime routine, but you must make them follow it consistently. Make sure you choose a simple routine that anyone can easily do, including their caregiver.

The routine should also be something you can do every night. It could be as simple as brushing their gums or teeth before bedtime so that they can associate it with sleep. You may also read something to them before you tuck them into bed at night. You can generate better results by starting to do the bedtime routine before they rub their eyes, as that shows they are already excessively tired.

Stay Calm During an Episode

Every time an episode of night terror strikes, note that the most practical thing you can do is remain calm. It is also advisable to wait a bit for your child to calm down. Never attempt to interact with them or intervene in the situation unless you are one hundred percent sure they are safe.

Keep in mind that while it can be frightening to witness a night terror, it is still not harmful to the child, so you do not have to be extremely worried. You should also stop yourself from waking them up during an episode. Just let them be.

Let them feel your presence without having to interrupt the entire process. Note that even if you try to wake them up, they will still not recognize you. You are even at risk of experiencing more agitation if you try comforting them.

Talk to Them in the Morning

An episode of nighttime terror is something your child cannot remember once they wake up in the morning. It is still helpful to talk with them about it upon waking up.

The goal is to figure out if they have certain worries that are causing the episodes. Just make sure you do the talk somewhat positively. Avoid discussing it in a frightening way, as it might only cause more anxiety on their part.

Offer Comfort and Security

You can also try offering them something comforting and finding out if such an object reduces the frequency of the nighttime fears. It could be a toy that they find comforting.

The goal is to let them hold something that will make them feel protected and secure every time they sleep at night. That way, they will become less prone to experiencing nighttime terrors.

This comfort-inducing item can also come in the form of a night-light. While working through your child's nighttime fears, switch to using a night-light, which is dimmer than a normal light. It should provide dim light while also having a warm and soft hue.

This type of night-light is a big help for kids with night terrors. Avoid bright and blue lights as these may hinder melatonin production in your toddler's brain, preventing them from getting drowsy during bedtime.

Reduce Stress

Try to find out if something is stressing them out. Remember that stress is one of the major reasons kids experience nighttime fears. If you think that your child is stressed, find out the source. Your goal is to lower their stress levels so that they can sleep peacefully every night with no episodes of nighttime fears and terrors.

Moreover, make sure they get enough rest every time. Avoid making them excessively tired. Avoid enabling them to stay up too late. Otherwise, this overtiredness may make them more prone to experiencing more frequent and longer night terror episodes.

Dress Them in Comfortable Light Clothes for Bedtime

This tip is more on preventing the nighttime fears and terrors from taking place. Let them wear light and comfortable clothes before sleeping. Note that you are just increasing your child's likelihood of experiencing night terrors if you dress them in heavy or thick clothes that could cause overheating. Aside from letting them dress lightly, make sure you also tuck them into bed and under a light blanket, giving them the choice of having a larger cover available should they become cold.

Make the Room Conducive for Sleep

Make sure their bedroom is comfortable enough and conducive to sleep. Remove anything in the room that might disrupt their sleep, such as electronic screens and bothersome noises. Also, make sure the room is completely safe to lower the risk of them getting hurt whenever they have an episode.

You should also remember that nighttime terrors usually happen to kids that are too warm. With that in mind, make sure the temperature in their room is always between around 62.6 to 69.8 degrees Fahrenheit (17 to 21 degrees Celsius). The room temperature should be cool enough that they will remain comfortable throughout their sleep.

When Should You Contact a Doctor?

You have to make sure you visit the child's pediatrician, especially if you think the night terrors are no longer normal. Set up an appointment with the pediatrician to determine if your child is suffering from any problem causing the night terrors. It could be that they have certain health problems, like adenoids, enlarged tonsils, or sleep apnea.

By visiting their doctor, your child can undergo the appropriate tests necessary in ruling out unwanted health problems. For instance, for enlarged tonsils and adenoids, a child can undergo a procedure that will remove those problematic parts that obstruct sleep. Once removed, you can expect them to sleep more soundly every night.

In case your child's night terrors and fears become too frequent, the best thing you can do is record anything related to each episode in a sleep diary. Do this for one or two weeks to monitor all factors connected to the problem.

Among those things that you should record are your child's bedtime schedule, the number of hours they sleep every night, the number of hours they wake up at night, how long each episode lasts, and the specific item they use for comfort or to fall asleep.

Record the number of naps they have every day, as well as potential triggers of the night terrors. The sleep diary will be a big help to you and your child's pediatrician, especially with determining the common triggers of each episode. If the night terrors continue, no matter how much effort you put in to stop them, visiting the pediatrician is the best thing you can do.

Moreover, consulting a doctor is wise if your child suffers from any of the following concerning sleep terrors:

- Significant increase in frequency
- Disrupts not only your baby's sleep but your sleep and that of others
- Results in injury or other safety concerns
- Causes daytime symptoms associated with problems in functioning and excessive sleepiness
- Does not have any sign of stopping; for example, if the sleep terrors continue as your child reaches teenage years

With the help of a pediatrician, you can identify the cause of the problem. They can even recommend a sleep specialist who can help your child experience better sleep quality. If the episodes start to affect your child's daily activities, i.e., their performance in school and relationships with family and friends, their doctor may prescribe low doses of tricyclic antidepressants or benzodiazepines—though this is rare. In most cases, night terrors naturally die down as your toddler gets older.

Remember that the doctor often diagnoses night terrors regarding your child's medical history and the result of a physical exam. If they suspect other health issues, additional tests may be given, including an EEG, a noninvasive test that measures your child's brain waves.

This helps to determine if your child has an ailment that could cause seizures. Another test is a polysomnography, a sleep examination designed to determine if there is a breathing disorder. If your doctor does not find any major health concerns, you do not have to worry too much. It usually means your child's case is normal and that the disorder will eventually go away on its own.

Chapter 7: Nightmares and Bedwetting

Another factor that might be a hindrance to successful toddler sleep training is having nightmares. If your toddler often has terrifying nightmares, expect them to wake up in the middle of the night and have a hard time going back to sleep. Their nightmares may also result in other interferences when it comes to falling back to sleep—one of which is bedwetting. How can you deal with the two things simultaneously? This chapter provides you with plenty of helpful answers.

Nightmares in Toddlers Defined

Everyone, regardless of age, experiences nightmares. The problem is that their effects seem to be worse for toddlers and children. If your toddler has nightmares often, these realistic yet unpleasant and bad dreams may have a huge negative impact on their sleep.

It is characterized as a bad dream because it often involves an imagined threat or danger. This means their nightmare may be all about a scary or dangerous situation. Nightmares even come with disturbing images, figures, and themes. These may come in the form of ghosts, scary animals, bad people, and monsters.

Fear of being injured and a complete loss of control are also among the usual themes when your child has a nightmare. While a nightmare happens now and then for many kids, you can expect it to be a more common occurrence among preschoolers or kids around three to six years.

This is because it is the age when kids' imaginations are highly active. It is also the time when they have already developed normal fears that might cause them to have bad dreams.

What Makes Nightmares Different from Night Terrors?

Nightmares are not the same as night terrors. Night terrors cause a child to experience episodes of extreme panic. The child may be confused, cry out, and move around. Waking the child during a night terror is often difficult, and the child rarely remembers the dream that caused the terror.

Note that nightmares in toddlers differ from nighttime fears that were discussed in the previous chapter. One thing that distinguishes nightmares from nighttime fears is the child's level of awareness. This is because a nightmare is something your toddler can remember. If your toddler is more verbal, there is even a chance for them to talk about it with you.

They can discuss it with you since they can usually recall the entire experience vividly. As for night terrors, you cannot expect toddlers and kids to remember the episode upon waking up. Another thing that makes the two different is the time when they take place. You can expect night terrors to disturb your child's sleep early into their sleep, usually after one to two hours.

It could come in the form of partial awakening, so they look like they have woken up, though not completely. Nightmares, on the other hand, often happen during the later parts of the night. You can expect nightmares to disrupt your toddler's sleep after midnight. Nightmares are also different from night terrors in the sense that the former may cause your child to wake up.

They may even cry incessantly and look for you for reassurance and help to calm down. These nightmares may also cause your toddler to experience difficulties going back to sleep. It should be noted that while all people experience nightmares, this situation could be more problematic for toddlers and kids.

This is because while they can recall what happens to them while they are having a nightmare, they still do not understand how to properly explain the problem. Some may find it extremely challenging to discuss the problem, especially if their language skills are not fully developed.

If you are a parent with a child who often has nightmares, part of their sleep training should involve learning how to deal with such issues at night. You will have an easier time dealing with the problem if you know exactly what is causing the nightmare.

By knowing the actual cause, you can use the most appropriate approach to handle nightmares whenever they happen, and you can ensure they do not stop your child from having a peaceful sleep every night.

Common Causes of Nightmares in Toddlers

Identifying the cause of your child's nightmare should be one of the first few steps you should undertake toward solving this specific problem affecting their sleep. One thing to note when trying to identify the exact cause of toddler nightmares is they are usually created by the specific part of your brain responsible for REM sleep.

Among these parts are those vital to processing emotional experiences and those responsible for memory. The problem with nightmares is that they seem real and vivid, which is why their effects can be extremely distressing to your child. Moreover, remember these are normal during the growth and development stage of any child.

However, certain causes can help you guide your toddler or child in dealing with nightmares more efficiently, making it possible for them to enjoy a good sleep still afterward. Sometimes, your child will have nightmares because of hearing or seeing something upsetting during the day.

Another likely cause is a traumatic experience. It might cause fears, leading them to dream about it at night. Your child's nightmares may also arise from their development. Sometimes it happens as a way for them to cope with certain changes in their life.

It could be because of starting school, living with parents who got remarried or divorced, or a recent move to a new place or neighborhood. Nightmares may also result from psychological and genetic factors. Aside from that, they are common among kids who have depression, intellectual disability, and certain ailments affecting the brain. Other potential causes of toddler nightmare you should be aware of include:

- High fever
- Certain medications during or after treatment
- Stress and conflicts
- Excessive tiredness
- Insufficient sleep
- Irregular sleep routines
- Seizures
- Sleep-disordered breathing, particularly caused by sleep apnea

Sleep apnea is probably the most important to identify among the causes of nightmares in toddlers. That is because those who have sleep apnea will not only have nightmares but also display other symptoms, like teeth grinding, snoring, and bedwetting.

Kids with sleep apnea may also have sweaty and restless sleep and tend to use their mouths when breathing. They display growth, attention, and behavioral problems during the day. If your child is diagnosed with sleep apnea, it could be one of the major causes of their nightmares. It is important to treat it by reversing its symptoms, which usually includes resolving nightmares too.

Dealing with Nightmares in Toddlers

Once you have identified what specifically causes your toddler to have seemingly incessant nightmares, it is time to craft a few solutions that will certainly help you and them to deal with each episode. You have to seriously consider finding ways to make your child handle their nightmares more effectively, especially if those disrupt their sleep.

Meaning that even with their night terrors and nightmares, if you train your toddler to sleep independently, it will become easier. The following are just some of the most effective ways for you and your child to handle their nightmares:

• *Make sure they get enough sleep* – One way to lessen the frequency of your toddler or child's nightmares is to make them sleep the required number of hours for their age. They should get adequate sleep and maintain a regular bedtime routine and schedule. This could be a big help toward cutting down the intensity and frequency of their nightmares.

• *Identify your child's fears* – Find out what your child is afraid of. Talk with them to find the bits and pieces of information that will let you pinpoint their fear, especially if they are still at an age when they cannot clearly relay their message. Ask open-ended questions, so they can let you know the specific things that scare them at bedtime.

Avoid making fun of their fears because even the most trivial and funniest things for you are extremely real for them. Learn more about their fears, as doing so can help you find ways to reassure them.

• *Avoid making them believe the imaginative creatures in their head exist* – Never say things that can cause your child to believe the frightening creatures they imagined are real. This means you should avoid telling them that you will save them from it because doing so may only confirm it indeed exists. Try to make them realize that what they're afraid of is just a figment of their imagination and is not true; otherwise, you won't be able to comfort them.

• *Create fun and happy bedtime routines* – This means you should develop routines before bedtime that can make your child feel happy and at peace. Avoid exposing them to scary TV shows, movies, and music thirty to 60 minutes before their bedtime schedule.

Also, do not read frightening bedtime stories or expose them to anything that might be upsetting. You should be able to calm them down and soothe them before falling asleep, so their experience throughout the night will also be peaceful. A calm mind can contribute to preventing nightmares.

Some of those fun and happy bedtime routines that make your child feel relaxed and eliminate worry are putting on their chosen pair of pajamas, brushing their teeth, letting them play with their favorite stuffed toy, and reading a fun and relaxing story to them. You should also use this time to cuddle before you tuck them into bed. It is a big help toward making them feel secure.

• *Talk about their nightmares* – It is also advisable for you to discuss their nightmares during the daytime. Your goal should be to identify a theme or pattern, especially if the nightmares become too frequent. If you have identified a theme or pattern, maybe something is bothering your child.

Maybe they are dealing with stressors that cause them to have nightmares whenever they sleep. Discuss such stressors and try to work together in lessening or fully eliminating them.

• *Create a cozy bedroom conducive for sleeping* – Your goal here should be to create the most reassuring and safest sleep environment for them. Their bedroom needs to be designed in a way that will make them feel safe. It should let them calm down, recharge, and reinvigorate them for another busy day.

One thing you can do to make their bedroom conducive for sleeping is to add a night-light to provide a sense of security. However, it is crucial to go for a night-light with a warm hue. It should not have any blue light either. Also, set the most comfortable room temperature appropriate for sleeping.

Make sure that no disturbing noises will distract them once you close their door. You may also want to invest in a white noise machine and put it in their room to block external and unwanted sounds, which will allow them to sleep peacefully.

• *Offer reassurance* – This tip is something that you should do whenever your child has nightmares. Remember that nightmares can be frightening and unfamiliar territory for kids. With that in mind, you need to reassure and comfort your toddler or child whenever they have just experienced a nightmare.

Tell them that it is just a bad dream. It is not true and will never hurt them. They may think their dream took place somewhere. In that case, help them to understand that it is all make-believe. Let them know that it did not and will never happen.

Also, make sure that you constantly remind them that you are just in the next room. Reassure them that you will always be there to keep them safe from harm. It can also reassure them if you label what they just went through.

While it is important to make them realize that nightmares are not real, avoid dismissing or belittling their experience. What you can do is share with them that you also had nightmares when you were their age—and sometimes still do.

It can somewhat reassure them that someone understands what they are going through, and they're not the only one dealing with it.

- *Comfort them in their room* - Avoid leaving your child all alone right after they have just woken up from a nightmare. Spend a few minutes with them to comfort them by providing extra cuddles. Providing this comfort can make them feel safe. However, you must make these comforting gestures in their bedroom instead of yours.

Even if they run into your room after a nightmare, make it a point to go back to their room and comfort them in there. This tip is vital for sleep training as it can make them realize that their bedroom is as safe and secure as yours. If you practice keeping them in their bedroom even when they have a nightmare, you can prevent them from developing a nightly habit of sleeping beside you in your room.

- *Divert their imagination* - Right after a nightmare, it would not be surprising for your child to imagine the worst out of the situation. In that case, you can help them by diverting their imagination. Guide them to a scenario that could have given their dream a positive result.

You may also turn the experience into a fun game that will stir their imagination. For instance, if their dream is about a monster chasing them, make them imagine what it would be like to discover that the monster was actually their friend who needs their help. This will surely stir their imagination. It can even remove their fears since they will try to act as the savior in the situation.

- *Let them find ways to overcome nightmares* - Teach them a few ways to get over nightmares creatively. Your goal is to help your child outgrow such bad dreams, so they will not feel so frightened that they can no longer sleep again on their own.

You can make them overcome nightmares by reading exciting and calming stories after each episode. Another tip is to let them draw pictures of the nightmare, tear it apart, and throw it away; doing so can make your child realize that they have full control over their nightmares, so there is nothing to be afraid of.

In most cases, treating nightmares is unnecessary. It is because most of these experiences resolve over time without any intervention. However, if your child's sleep quality is drastically affected, you need to do something about it. You can use the tips mentioned above to help them overcome nightmares and train them gradually to sleep on their own, even after a scary dream.

How to Avoid Bedwetting

Bedwetting is common among toddlers and children who have just experienced a nightmare. Your child may wet their bed as a result of the fear brought on by a bad dream. The goal is to avoid bedwetting because the discomfort from it may make sleep training even more challenging as they will struggle to fall back asleep again.

You can lower the risk of them bedwetting after a nightmare with the help of these simple tips:

- *Reduce fluid intake at night* – There is a lower chance of your toddler or child wetting the bed if you lessen their fluid intake a couple of hours before bedtime. Try to shift their schedule for fluid intake. Give them fluids earlier in the day so that you can lower it at night, especially close to bedtime.

- *Set bathroom schedules* – Make your child develop the habit of urinating on a schedule. For instance, encourage them to go to the bathroom to pee every two hours. You should also let them do so before bedtime.

- *Get rid of anything that might irritate their bladder* - Make sure you do not expose your child to anything that might irritate their bladder at night. This means you have to eliminate anything that contains caffeine, like cocoa and chocolate.

Another alternative tip is to lessen their intake of sweeteners and citrus juices, and anything that contains dyes or unnatural colorings and artificial flavoring. Those things might irritate their bladder, making them more prone to wetting the bed at even a minor trigger.

- *Use pull-ups or diapers at night* - Do this even if they are already wearing the usual underwear during the daytime. If your child objects to wearing diapers again at night, you can put it on once they fall asleep. Another alternative is a pair of disposable training pants. A rubber sheet designed to protect their mattress is also a big help.

One more important tip is to avoid making your child feel bad about bedwetting. Do not punish them as it will only make them feel more frustrated, especially if it only happens because of their nightmares.

Instead of blaming them or making them feel more uncomfortable and guilty, let them know that it happens now and then, and both of you can fix it. Encourage them by telling them that they can prevent bedwetting incidents in the future, even if they happen because of a frightening nightmare.

Chapter 8: Sleepwalking and Sleep Talking

Another challenge that you may encounter when training your toddler to sleep on their own is the tendency to sleepwalk and to talk in their sleep. This is because both sleepwalking and sleep talking disturb your child's slumber. The problem is, if they either sleepwalk or sleep talk and then wake up in the process, they may find it extremely challenging to sleep again.

Though, one thing to observe is that these are normal occurrences. In fact, both happen to about thirty percent of toddlers and kids. With that said, either or both of the two can significantly impact your child's sleep, so it is essential to learn about sleepwalking and sleep talking as much as possible.

It is also crucial to learn what you can do to avoid it. Moreover, it helps to find out if any warning signs suggest needed help from a medical professional. That way, you or their caregiver can take immediate and appropriate action.

What Should You Know About Sleepwalking in Kids?

Sleepwalking—also called somnambulism—involves your child's purposeful walking movements that take place while they are in a sleep-like state. This behavior is categorized as parasomnia, a sleep disorder category that encompasses abnormal behaviors and movements during sleep.

Sleepwalking in toddlers and kids is characterized by them getting up even during their sleep while having no awareness of the action. You can often see this situation affecting kids around four to eight years old, but sometimes toddlers experience it too. Most of those who sleepwalk start doing so one or two hours after they fall into a deep sleep.

Each sleepwalking episode lasts for around five to fifteen minutes. Even though sleepwalking is not usually harmful to children and most outgrow the behavior, you still need to know that it is potentially harmful if you do not address the problem.

For instance, there is a risk of your child getting injured when they sleepwalk. With that in mind, you and their caregiver should work together to protect them from potential injuries. One way to do so is to figure out the specific factors that make your child more prone to sleepwalking.

You must pinpoint the cause of the sleepwalking so you can take the right action. Factors that might lead to sleepwalking are:

- Inadequate sleep
- Extreme fatigue or tiredness
- Irregular sleeping schedules, habits, and routines
- Staying in a new and different sleep environment
- Anxiety
- Fever or other illness

- Medications they are taking, like stimulants, antihistamines, and sedatives

If your family members have a history of sleepwalking, be aware that it might also contribute to your child having episodes of it. Each episode differs, but in most cases, your toddler or child will get out of bed or sit on their bed and then walk around their room. It often happens for less than ten minutes.

There are also instances when the sleepwalking episode will include your child putting on clothes, roaming or walking around the entire house, and opening doors. They may open their eyes even if they are still asleep. Their open eyes are also often accompanied by a glassy-eyed and glazed look.

Do not expect a clear answer if you have plans to ask them about what happened when they wake up in the morning. This is because your child cannot recall the sleepwalking episode once they fully wake up.

Also, be mindful that your toddler or child may display other actions and behaviors linked to the condition other than the most common sign of sleepwalking—which is walking while asleep. Other symptoms your toddler may show if they have the condition are:

- Sitting up while in bed and doing certain movements repeatedly
- Walking around the room or house
- Moving clumsily
- Not answering even if you are talking to them
- Mumbling or talking while asleep
- The tendency to urinate in inappropriate areas
- Doing repetitive or routine behaviors, like closing and opening the doors

Another thing to remember about sleepwalking is that while it is common and happens naturally in kids, sometimes it indicates an underlying condition. Conditions that might be linked to sleepwalking are sleep apnea, migraines, head injuries, restless leg syndrome, and night terrors.

How to Deal with Sleepwalking in Toddlers and Kids

If you think your child's case is normal and does not relate to any other major health concerns but are still worried about their safety during each episode, you have to train yourself to do things that will lessen the sleepwalking tendencies.

Moreover, you have to do something about it if you feel like their sleep is already drastically affected. Note that if you do not take action, even if their case is normal, you can experience major difficulties and challenges during their sleep training.

Here are a few practical pieces of advice for you and your toddler's caregiver that should make the child less prone to sleepwalking and guarantee their safety during each episode:

Implement Safety Measures at Home

Note that your toddler or child's safety will be compromised during every sleepwalking episode as they will most likely roam around the house, not fully aware of what they are doing. When they do that, they're at risk of getting injured. That said, it is advisable to implement safety measures around your house.

Among the safety measures that you and their caregiver should try to do are:

- Keeping the doors and windows closed and locked every night
- Getting rid of breakable and sharp items around the bed

- Getting rid of all tripping hazards, not only in your child's room but also the entire house
- Installing window and door alarms
- Putting locks in places that your child cannot easily reach
- Putting on safety gates in doorways and at the front part of stairs
- Ensuring that keys are out of your child's reach
- Preventing your child from sleeping in a bunk bed
- Turning down the hot water heater's temperature to lower their risk of getting burned

Your main goal should be to create a safe and secure home that is sleepwalker-proof. It also helps to hang a bell on their bedroom door, alerting you or their caregiver whenever the child sleepwalks and gets out of their room.

Set an Early Bedtime

This tip is a huge help if your goal is to prevent your child from sleepwalking in the first place. Keep in mind that one of the major causes of sleepwalking, especially in toddlers and children, is excessive fatigue. It can cause your child not only to sleepwalk but also to experience other sleep problems, like nightmares and night terrors.

You can prevent the fatigue that might trigger their sleepwalking by setting up an earlier bedtime and sticking to it. You may set it up thirty minutes to one hour before their usual schedule. The good thing about this tip is that it also helps to improve excessive sleepiness.

You should also try pairing up their early bedtime with relaxing routines. You can create a regular nap and sleep schedule, both for daytime and nighttime. Other routines that will make them think it is already close to bedtime are brushing their teeth, changing into their favorite sleepwear, and listening to bedtime stories or soothing music.

Never Wake Them Up During a Sleepwalking Episode

If you have a sleepwalker, make sure to avoid waking them up every time they have an episode. It will be best for you to guide them back to bed instead. Keep in mind that even if they are asleep, your child will most likely respond to the sound of your voice. Talk to them gently and calmly while guiding them back to their room or bed.

Practice Scheduled Awakenings

You may also wish to try the scheduled awakening technique if you have already identified the usual schedule when their sleepwalking happens. You can do this technique by waking up your child every night at around thirty minutes before the usual time of the sleepwalking episodes.

Try to do this technique every night for one month, and you will notice a significant reduction in the severity and frequency of the episodes. Make it a point to wake them up completely—one where they can hold a conversation. One issue with this technique, though, is that it can lead to sleep deprivation.

With that in mind, ensure they have enough sleep during the daytime to make up for it. Also, try doing this for only a month or just until you notice the sleepwalking episodes dwindling.

Reduce Liquid Intake Before Bedtime

Liquid is vital for your child's health as it helps them stay hydrated. However, it can also cause trouble, especially if they are prone to sleepwalking. This is because having a full bladder can trigger sleepwalking episodes.

With that in mind, make sure to limit your child's liquid consumption at night. It is also advisable to eliminate any drink that contains caffeine. Moreover, it helps if you let them use the toilet before sleep. With that routine, they will have a lower chance of being disturbed by anything during sleep.

Build a Sleep-Friendly Room

Another important tip to prevent sleepwalking and ensure they get enough undisturbed sleep every night is to make their room as relaxing and sleep-friendly as possible. Your goal is to create a quiet, comfortable, and dim sleep environment. It can make them relax and feel the need to sleep.

Ensure that the bedroom's temperature is low—around 75 degrees Fahrenheit or 24 degrees Celsius is the ideal temperature. It also helps to pair this up with relaxing routines, like deep breathing and a warm bath. That way, your child's mind will be conditioned to sleep peacefully without being disturbed by anything, even a sleepwalking episode.

When to Seek Medical Help

There is a possibility of a connection between sleepwalking and other possible ailments and conditions, so you and your toddler's caregiver must be vigilant in recognizing the behavior displayed by your child. You need to observe the child, especially during their sleepwalking episodes. Consider contacting a doctor if your child's sleepwalking episodes happen more frequently.

You may also need to seek professional medical help if you notice your child has a higher risk of injuring themselves or those around them every time they sleepwalk. Another scenario that warrants a doctor's help is if the sleepwalking episodes do not seem to end and continue as the toddler grows older.

You may also need to consult a doctor if you and your child's caregiver notice the following in your child:

- Sleepwalking episodes that start disturbing the sleep of other people in the household
- Extreme sleepiness during daytime
- Over two sleepwalking episodes every night

- The tendency to gasp for breath or snore loudly along with sleepwalking
- Bedwetting during sleepwalking episodes

Just relay the alarming signs and symptoms your child displays during sleepwalking episodes to your chosen doctor. You can then expect them to recommend a specialist sleep center, a place where your child's sleep history and your sleep pattern will be discussed.

If necessary, your doctor will arrange sleep examinations or studies. These studies' goal is to rule out other conditions and ailments that may be causing the episodes, like restless leg syndrome and sleep apnea. In the sleep study, your child will be asked to sleep in a sleep laboratory for a night.

Here, electrodes will be attached to various parts of your child's body. The main objective is to measure your child's brain waves, breathing, heart rate, leg and eye movements, blood oxygen level, and muscle tension. Your child will also be recorded on the camera while they are sleeping.

This study is often conducted if there is a high chance your child is suffering from a more serious condition. For troublesome cases of sleepwalking, your chosen doctor may also do scheduled awakening, a technique that keeps track of your child's sleep for several nights. It helps them to figure out the specific time when the episode often occurs.

Once the usual schedule of each episode is detected, your child will be roused from their sleep around fifteen minutes before such a schedule. It is a big help in resetting your child's sleep cycle and keeping sleepwalking behaviors, especially the more dangerous ones, under control.

Although rare, there are also times when the doctor will recommend the intake of certain medications—one of which is clonazepam. Clonazepam refers to a benzodiazepine medication used in suppressing one's nervous system. If taking the medication, the child will be less prone to getting up and roaming around while asleep.

Make sure to use this medication only in severe cases, though. Remember: It can produce side effects, so talk about it carefully with a pediatrician. Ask whether its benefits outweigh the risks and side effects, and if the medication is indeed right for your child. However, in the majority of sleepwalking cases, the use of medication is not necessary.

What Do You Need to Know About Sleep Talking?

If your child sleepwalks, there is also a tendency that this episode is accompanied by sleep talking. It often occurs if you notice your toddler or child talking, crying, moaning, or laughing even when asleep. Similar to sleepwalking episodes, your child is unaware that they talk during sleep. They will not also recall it once they wake up.

Sometimes, your child's sleep-talking episodes encompass words and phrases you can discern as well as complete sentences. However, there are cases when they talk complete nonsense. Whenever they talk during sleep, you will notice them sounding like themselves or talking using another voice. The things they are talking about can also be linked to past conversations and memories, or they may not be connected to anything.

It is important to consider that while sleep talking is usually genetic and comes with sleepwalking episodes, excessive fatigue and inadequate sleep can also trigger it. Moreover, your child may sleep talk because of stress, and that is why you should set a consistent and relaxing bedtime routine for them.

Just like the things you can do to lessen sleepwalking episodes, you also need to make sure your child gets enough quality and undisturbed sleep—around eleven to fourteen hours to prevent them from talking during sleep. Furthermore, remember that sleep talking usually accompanies night terrors, nightmares, sleep apnea, fever, and other vivid dreams.

You have to closely observe your child to find out if their case is still mild or could be considered sufficiently serious enough to be associated with an underlying condition. You can consider their condition mild if they sleep talk no more than once a week. On the other hand, if it happens each night for one whole month or more, be warier because it can be considered a more serious and pronounced case.

Talk with their pediatrician or doctor about it, and do not forget to ask the expert what to do to handle the case. It is even more important to have it treated if you find that your child's sleep talking is disturbing other members of your household or disruptive in some other way.

What Can You Do About Sleep Talking?

Dealing with sleep talking episodes in children is quite like the ones used to tackle sleepwalking. Tips you can apply are establishing regular sleeping schedules and routines, setting up scheduled awakenings, and ensuring your child gets enough sleep. You can perform those techniques together with the following to further improve its ability to reduce the frequency and severity of sleep talking:

• *Remove all forms of distraction during bedtime* – This includes gadgets, unnecessary noise, blue light, or anything that might prevent them from falling asleep on time. By removing distractions, your child has a greater chance of getting sufficient quality sleep.

• *Practice good sleeping hygiene* – Sleep hygiene refers to practices designed to improve your child's ability to sleep soundly. Among those you can include in their sleep hygiene are setting a relaxing and comfortable temperature in their bedroom and removing lamps producing bright lights close to their bed.

- *Prevent them from eating spicy, greasy, and fatty foods before bedtime* - Make sure they do not drink carbonated drinks either. These unhealthy foods and drinks can cause indigestion, thereby disturbing their sleep and making them more prone to sleep talking.

- *Make sure their bedroom receives enough sunlight during the day* - It should also have enough darkness at night. With that, your child has a higher chance of retaining a healthy cycle for sleeping and awakening.

- *Encourage them to exercise* - Make sure they have enough physical activities or exercise during the day. Good activities include swimming, cycling, and running—however, at this age, this kind of activity will need to be supervised. You may also want to get them involved in sports. Encouraging activity and exercise can significantly improve their sleep quality, translating to a lower chance of sleepwalking and sleep talking.

Just like sleepwalking, sleep talking is often harmless and a natural occurrence in kids. You can even expect your child to outgrow it soon, but if you notice that their symptoms are severe or their condition seems to persist longer than usual, seek the help of your doctor or a sleep specialist.

You can rely on medical professionals to diagnose your child's underlying conditions and issues and subsequently manage them if necessary. They can also guide you on your toddler's sleep training journey, making it as smooth as possible, and helping you remove issues, such as sleepwalking and sleep talking.

Chapter 9: Setting a Sleep Schedule

Have you finally resolved and addressed the issues affecting your child's sleep, like co-sleeping, sleepwalking, sleep talking, and night feeding? Then it is time to develop a sleep schedule for them. The good thing about putting a sleep schedule in place and sticking to it is that it can give your toddler more stability and confidence.

Besides that, your life as a parent and that of the child's caregiver(s) will become much easier. The ultimate secret to setting up a successful sleep schedule is to combine comfort, fun, and structure.

Once you have eliminated all the other obstacles and issues that affect your child's sleep quality, practice the schedule right away. This helps your toddler familiarize themselves with the new routine.

Once they get used to it, you are also assured that they will be more than willing to make adjustments to the schedule as they get older, so it can fit their specific needs.

When Should You Start Setting Up a Sleep Schedule?

Note that as soon as your baby hits two or three months, you can try sleep training them and setting up a regular sleep schedule as this is the period when their internal clock becomes more predictable. When that happens, you can begin to implement basic schedules that fit newborns.

At around three to six months, you will notice their bedtime, wake-up times, and naptimes falling at similar times daily. You can use this information to anticipate the specific times when they naturally feel sleepy, thereby making it possible for you to put them down when they are already drowsy while still awake.

This is necessary as it can train them and help develop a useful skill—falling asleep independently.

What is the Ideal Sleep Schedule for Toddlers?

The answer to this will depend on the specific amount of sleep your child needs. For instance, toddlers need a total of eleven to fourteen hours daily. It should also include naptimes of around one to two hours every day. Also, keep in mind that while toddlers' sleep schedules vary, most of them tend to sleep better when you tuck them in bed by around 7:30 to 8:00 in the evening.

This is because most kids who sleep before 9:00 in the evening tend to fall asleep quicker. They also have a lower risk of waking up during the night, thereby allowing them to get better rest and sleep for several hours. In that case, you can also anticipate your child to wake up at around 6:00 to 7:00 in the morning.

Some toddlers even rise earlier. If your child is an early riser, waking up before 6:00 in the morning, you can rest assured there are still ways for you to make them hit their snooze button. For instance, you can put their favorite toys near them so that they can reach them easily.

If you do that, they will be less likely to call you right away. You may also want to install room-darkening shades designed to prevent natural light from coming in. It can contribute to your child thinking they still need to sleep more until their scheduled wake-up time.

Effective Tips for Setting Up a Sleep Schedule for Toddlers

One important thing you have to think about when it comes to toddlers is that they are notorious for resisting sleep. It is why you really must look for tips and techniques that will let them follow through on a healthy sleep schedule. Your goal is to establish healthy sleeping habits and make sure they follow them.

One way to achieve that is to have consistent naptimes and bedtimes daily. Aside from letting your toddler get the required number of sleeping hours, you can also expect to have an easier time sleep training them. Moreover, once they have a consistent sleep-wake cycle, your life will also start to become easier again with the predictable patterns and a higher likelihood of you getting enough rest and sleep.

For you to have an easier time setting up a sleep schedule for your toddler or child, it is highly recommended to apply the following tips:

Set a Sleep Schedule Based on Your Toddler's Cues

As often as you can, begin sleep training as early as possible. It does not mean that you should already start setting a sleep schedule when you still have a newborn, as you cannot expect them to follow it yet. With that said, you can start trying to modify their internal clock as early as two months.

Your goal is to create a sleep and eating timetable depending on their personality and snoozing habits. Remember to base your child's sleep schedule on their cues. Find out about the specific signs that clearly indicate when they are sleepy. Observe them and determine the usual things they do whenever they begin to feel tired.

For instance, it might be incessant crying, being fussy, or constant rubbing of the eyes. Those actions indicate they already want to take a nap or sleep at night. Your goal here is to familiarize yourself with your child's behaviors and cues, as those will help you craft the most suitable sleep schedule for them—one they can easily follow through on.

Have a Sleep Log

Another thing you can do to establish a good sleep schedule is to have a sleep log. You have to record everything related to their sleep. Doing that will give you a clear idea of the usual time they sleep, making it possible for you to schedule their bedtime and naptime accordingly.

The sleep log will also let you know about their waking windows and sleeping patterns. With that, you will know how much they can handle being awake and the specific time they need to sleep. Note that every baby or toddler is unique, so you have to create a sleep schedule that suits them well.

Set Up a Wake-Up Time

Your toddler should be able to start their day with a set wake-up schedule. As indicated earlier, some toddlers rise early—around 6:00 to 7:00 in the morning. If you notice they wake up later than that, avoid waking them up earlier. Note that you are still starting to set up the most appropriate routines and schedules, so it helps if you let them decide when they can comfortably wake up.

If they already have a scheduled pattern for waking up, try to stick to it because that is more comfortable for them. It is also advisable to let them spend around fifteen minutes slowly waking up on their own.

Let them play for a while in their crib during this time before preparing them for the day. It would be best for you to try waiting until 7:00 in the morning to facilitate the beginning of their day.

Incorporate routines that will clearly let them know it is already daytime. For instance, you may want to spend around half an hour dressing them and brushing their teeth and hair. Other routines you can incorporate here include washing their face and letting them use the toilet.

Schedule Breakfast

You may also want to set up a schedule for their breakfast. Depending on their needs, it may be more appropriate to set the breakfast time before brushing their teeth and getting dressed. It is a more suitable routine if they tend to wake up hungry. In that case, it would be best to feed them first so that they will be more likely to cooperate with you once it is time to bathe, brush their teeth, and get dressed.

Make it a point to prepare a light breakfast for them. It should be something they can easily digest. Moreover, try to shorten the amount of time they spend eating breakfast—as this should take no more than half an hour. This will give them more time to play later in the morning.

Include Morning and Afternoon Naps

Naptimes should form part of your child's daily routine as they provide times when they can reinvigorate themselves. It is important to note that not including naps in their daily schedule may affect their sleep quality in the evening. It may also be harder for you to set up a more consistent sleep schedule without letting them nap consistently.

If they are already up by 7:00 a.m., consider setting their naptime around 9:30 to 10:00 in the morning. It should take at least an hour. However, keep in mind that as they grow older, they may also outgrow their morning nap. Do not force them to nap if you feel like they have already outgrown this routine in the morning.

In that case, you may want to fill up their supposed-to-be morning nap with quiet and relaxing activities. You can let them look at books, listen to audiobooks, or play. Allowing them enough quiet time will recharge them, giving them more energy to do more physical activities later in the day.

Set up an afternoon nap schedule for them too. Schedule it after lunch, preferably during the resting period at around 2:00 in the afternoon. As much as possible, do not expect the nap to last for over two hours. Allowing them to nap too late and too long may affect their ability to sleep on time at night.

Establish Routines for the Late Afternoon

You should also include late afternoon routines in your child's daily schedule if you want them to fall asleep at night more easily. Plan these activities after their afternoon nap. It could be a light snack and outdoor activities. It is highly recommended to let them play outdoors, like walking around the neighborhood or in a playground close to your home or letting them run outside in your yard.

Your goal is to let them move, which is good for their body, while also trying to let their energy dwindle before dinner. If you do that, you will have an easier time smoothly preparing them for dinner and bedtime. The fact that you are already trying to use all their energy through outdoor play will also increase their chance of sleeping on a set schedule.

Create Before Bed Routines

You should also establish routines your toddler can do before bedtime. Remember that the first parts of the sleep training will be challenging since you will have a hard time sticking to a consistent daily schedule. Fortunately, you can lessen such challenges by trying to create routines before bedtime.

All it takes is to ingrain such routines into your child's habits until they become used to doing them and associate them with sleeping. Once you begin the training, make it a point to stick to similar routines before bedtime and the same bedtime each night. As much as possible, let your toddler go to bed at around 8:00 in the evening. This is the perfect bedtime for toddlers to have adequate sleep.

The best way to handle the evening and prepare your child for bedtime is to let them play a bit after dinner. After a short playtime, let them do a relaxing activity. It could be reading a book or watching their favorite TV show. Another routine that they should associate with sleep is a nighttime snack (i.e., a glass of warm milk). You may also want to incorporate time for their warm and relaxing bath.

To further make them more accustomed to their bedtime and stick to it, add more relaxing routines, like reading a bedtime story to them or singing a calming and relaxing song. To make them relax even more, give them a comfort blanket or let their favorite toy lie next to them. With a security item close, like their favorite toy, you can expect them to fall asleep faster.

Mistakes to Avoid When Setting a Sleep Schedule for your Toddler

As a parent, it is normal for you to get confused during the sleep training process. It is especially true if you have a somewhat resistant toddler who is quite difficult to train when sticking to a consistent sleep schedule. To somewhat smooth out the process, here are the mistakes committed by other parents when setting up a sleep schedule for their kids:

• *Changing routines now and then* – Recognize that to make your toddler's sleep training a huge success, you need to be very consistent with the bedtime and naptime routines that you are trying to set in place. With that in mind, you have to avoid changing the routines you have already established from time to time.

Never do something like a trial-and-error when encouraging your kids to stick to bedtime routines. It is because doing so may only confuse your child, making it even harder and more challenging to train them to sleep independently. Once a routine is already established, stick to it, and follow it consistently.

• *Not paying attention to your toddler's cues* – Just like what has been indicated in one of the tips mentioned for setting up a sleep schedule, you need to watch out for your toddler's cues. Try to set routines and a sleep schedule based on such cues.

Never make the mistake of establishing a routine based on what only fits your schedule. If you do that, you will miss out on sleep because they already send sleep cues earlier than you have anticipated based on your presently established routines.

• *Establishing too long bedtime routines* – Decide beforehand the amount of time that you can ideally spend on your child's bedtime routine every night. Make sure that it is not too long, though.

Keep in mind that if the routine you make your child follow every night lasts for more than an hour or two, putting them to sleep will be even harder. It would also be difficult for both of you to stick to the routine regularly.

Try to make your child's bedtime routines as short as possible. Go for those that are just enough to make them calm down and sleep faster.

• *Giving in to your toddler's desire to stay up late* – Make sure you do not commit the mistake other parents make by giving in to their kids' desire to stay up late. It could come in the form of letting your toddler play longer because you feel like you have had insufficient time with them due to your busy work schedule.

The problem with allowing them to stay up late and not stick to their usual bedtime schedule is that it can lead to them dealing with excessive tiredness. This can further result in crankiness and a refusal to sleep on time. They can also see you are flexible, which may cause problems in the future.

With that said, make it a point to stick to the sleep schedule you have already set. Ensure the bedtime is right for both of you so that you will not have problems following through on it.

• *Not removing all the distractions from the bedroom* - If you want to be truly successful in sleep training your toddler, you have to make sure that all distractions in their bedroom are eliminated once you have created a sleep schedule and commit to following it.

Some parents believe a great-looking mobile, quiet music, and nice night-light can greatly contribute to their kids quickly falling asleep. It is not the case all the time, though. Take your cues from your toddler's behavior.

In fact, there are instances when these items become distractions, causing toddlers to stay awake even if it is already long past their bedtime. With that said, try only to implement the sleep schedule and routine you created once their bedroom is already distraction-free.

• *Sending mixed signals and messages about your toddler's sleeping spot* - Another mistake to avoid is making your toddler think their bedroom is not the only place where they can sleep. This means you should not let them climb into your bed several times every week, especially during those instances when they become extra fussy and cranky.

Bear in mind that if you let them think they can still share the bed with you, it might cause problems in the sleep technique you are trying to implement and send a mixed message to your toddler. It might confuse them, disrupting their sleep.

To avoid that from happening, be firm and make them follow specific guidelines on where they should sleep. Make them follow the sleep schedule you created by trying to end their nighttime visits.

Just make sure you gently explain to them the reasons why they need to stay and sleep in their bedroom the entire night. Implementing this sleep schedule without fail for a couple of weeks will surely help your child sleep independently without requiring the help of anyone, including you.

• *Not making gradual adjustments* – Remember that it will take a bit of time for your child to get used to the new sleeping routines and schedule. It is the reason why you must avoid expecting them to adjust right away. Do not make the mistake of rushing the process.

You have to let them adjust slowly. Understand that changing their sleep schedule overnight is impossible, so making minor and small changes gradually is what you must do. Make adjustments—for instance, through fifteen-minute increments—to the bedtime schedule until the specific bedtime you want your child to follow is reached.

Avoid these seven mistakes, and you will surely have a high chance of making your toddler stick to the bedtime or sleep schedule you already set up. Again, be consistent and firm when trying to make them follow the routines and new sleep schedule.

Running these similar activities every night sends messages and cues to their brain that it is already time for them to sleep. By establishing calming pre-bed routines and setting up an appropriate sleep schedule, your toddler will be able to wind down, promoting better sleep for them as well as a lower risk of having middle of the night awakenings.

Chapter 10: The Growing Toddler: Dealing with Change

One thing you should remember about toddlers and children is they tend to grow fast. This means their sleeping habits will also most likely change in the future. How can you help your growing toddler deal with the changes they will most likely encounter during their growth and development?

How can you help them adjust to various sleeping patterns and the transitions they need to make? The last chapter of this book aims to find answers to your questions so that you can guide your child toward dealing with all the changes that they may find confusing and alarming. It is especially true if the change involves getting separated from their parents as they transition into a bigger bed and a new bedroom.

Making Adjustments on Various Sleeping Routines and Habits

Depending on your toddler's or child's age, they may need to make constant adjustments to sleeping routines and habits. There is no need to make a drastic change. It would be best to make gradual changes—something your child will not notice right away to prevent the drama and other unnecessary and unwanted reactions.

Make sure you make adjustments to your growing child's routines based on their age and the specific amount of sleep they need at that particular time. For instance, at around six months old, they need to meet the daily required number of sleep hours, which is around ten to eleven hours.

Here, you have to incorporate two to three naps during the daytime, with the first two naps being around one and a half to two hours each. Train your child to have a shorter nap. Once they reach around nine months, expect them to need around ten to twelve hours of shut-eye. One of the major adjustments you have to make during this time is the elimination of night feeding.

You have to focus on completely weaning them and feeding solid foods, so they will no longer ask for night feeds. At this age, two naps—taking about one and a half to two hours each—during the daytime will be okay. Make sure not to set naptimes before 3:30 to 4:30 in the afternoon.

Ensure you introduce the habit of napping after lunch so that they will wake up by 3:00 p.m. That way, you can give them enough activities right after their nap, which will use all their energy and make them fully prepared for bed by around 7:00 to 9:00 in the evening.

You have to try introducing good sleeping habits, even just minor ones, to your child before they hit one-year-old. That way, making major adjustments regarding their sleep will be much easier moving forward.

Remember that once they get into toddlerhood, instilling new habits and routines will be much more challenging. This is because they will most likely resist new changes, so training them to follow even just minor bedtime routines before that can help.

One- to Two-year-old Routines

Upon reaching one year old, expect your child to be more active. They will also become more resistant and most likely want to do things their way, making it a bit harder to let them adjust to the changes in their sleep. During this age, one reminder is to make sure that they constantly receive around ten to twelve hours of sleep, including two naps with a duration of one to two hours each.

At one and a half years, they will need around eleven to twelve hours of sleep every night. It is also the time when you and your toddler will have to adjust naptimes because it will drop to just one during the day. To make it easier to stick to, set this one nap around lunchtime, allowing it to take around one and a half to two hours.

As for bedtime, make sure you set a consistent schedule for them to sleep and wake up. That way, they will not have a hard time adjusting to the routines. Note that your child can smoothly survive any major change in bedtime and sleeping routines if you set a regular bedtime.

Also, try to make bedtimes predictable. Help them sleep on time by preventing them from doing fun and exciting stuff that might only further raise their energy, like outdoor play. It would help if you also stopped feeding them with sugary snacks, drinks, and meals thirty minutes or so before bedtime.

It also helps if their dinner consists of foods containing carbs, like cereals or rice and bread. Let them drink milk at dinnertime too. Such foods can stimulate the production of melatonin, a hormone necessary for sleep. If you already give your child a little screen time, do not set it up close to bedtime.

This means turning off the TV, other gadgets, and screens one hour or so before their bedtime. You can further make them accustomed to bedtime by doing the following during that period:

- Brushing their teeth
- Changing into a new and clean diaper
- Turning their night light on - It can prevent them from feeling extremely upset if they wake up and realize they are all alone in the dark. Make sure to stay away from blue lights, and choose red and yellow night-lights.
- Tucking them into bed while they are still awake but already drowsy
- Letting them relax by reading a short story

With all these routines set, adjusting to new sleeping habits based on their age will be manageable.

Transitioning to a New and Big Bed

Some parents agree that the best time to start letting their kids transition to a newer and bigger bed is between one to two years old. You can also do the same for your child, but be prepared to make them feel safe and secure, even if you are no longer sharing the same bed or bedroom. Expect resistance during the transition since this is a huge change your child has to go through, but you can manage such a challenge with these simple tips:

Determine if They are Ready First

It is hard to resist the temptation of making your toddler move to a new bed and room as soon as they hit around one or two. However, avoid doing it right away without scrutinizing your child's readiness level because not all toddlers are ready to take the leap even when they reach such an age.

There are even those who only seem to be ready when they get close to three years old or so. It is mainly because toddlers are strongly attached to you, their crib, and their sleep associations. Those things make them feel safe and secure when it is time to go to bed. With those considerations in mind, avoid rushing the process.

The perfect time to transition them to a new bedroom is when you start noticing them asking for it. If possible, wait for them to show signs that they are ready before taking the big leap. You may also want to discuss it with them slowly. Explain how good it will be for them to have their own bed and room where they will have freedom and independence. Make sure your toddler never thinks of their bedroom as an area of punishment because this negative connection will disrupt your attempts to teach your toddler to go to bed peacefully in their room. If you need a timeout area, keep it away from the bedroom so that it will be a safe place for the child psychologically.

Pick the Right Toddler Bed

Make sure you are also very cautious when it comes to choosing your child's bed. They are sure to feel excited to transition if they see how great their toddler bed is. In this case, you have a couple of options—including a toddler bed resembling a smaller version of a twin bed.

You can go for one that comes in the form of a fire truck, princess castle, or race car. Your goal is to look for a concept and style your toddler will surely love, thereby enticing them to move to it.

Another choice is a twin bed with safety rails outfitted. The two are great options, so you can pick one based on your budget, the amount of space in your child's bedroom, and their temperament. Go for a sturdy and durable bed too. Remember that it is for a child that will most likely roll, jump, bounce, wiggle, and do other fun and exciting stuff.

You need to look for a bed capable of withstanding the daily use and abuse of most toddlers. Make sure the bed is low to the ground and has safety rails. It is necessary to prevent your child from getting injured due to falling accidentally. They can also easily get in and out of the toddler bed if it is low to the ground.

Allow Your Child to Participate in the Process

This means you should get them involved in the transition. For instance, you can make them choose the design for their toddler bed, so you can provoke their excitement and further encourage them to move into their new room. Allow them to choose the bedding and sheets too. You should also encourage them to customize their new room and bed. If you have a limited budget, just give them alternatives you can afford.

Customizing the room can be achieved by arranging their favorite toys and stuffed animals based on what they want. Whether you decide to go for a twin or toddler bed, make it a point to let your toddler participate during the selection process.

Reinforce New Bedtime Rules

If you have made your toddler agree to sleep in a new room or bed, it is highly likely they will love their newfound freedom and independence. This may make it hard for them to resist exploring and roaming around their new environment. It is not a good idea, though, especially if they tend to explore very close to bedtime.

With that in mind, you have to reinforce new bedtime rules to minimize their need to explore. One rule you may want to set in place is to schedule a last call or request for their favorite toy, water, or a trip to the bathroom before you finally tuck them into bed. Be firm and make them understand how important it is to follow the new rules.

Childproof the Home

When your child has to transition to a new bed and room, you have to begin reevaluating the childproofing methods you have set in place. Before making the transfer, find out if you need to set other safety measures and precautions in place that will guarantee your toddler's safety in case they end up adventuring at night.

One tip is to use safety gates to block all stairwells. Make it a point to lock the windows and all doors leading outdoors. Moreover, you have to make sure they cannot reach those areas where you keep harmful materials as well as certain medications and cleaning products. You can also have covers put on electrical outlets.

Childproofing your home, not just your toddler's bedroom, is especially important, especially if they are someone who loves to roam around and explore. It is all the more important if they tend to sleepwalk, making them more prone to getting injured.

Put Their New Stuff in the Proper Places

Note that being consistent is extremely necessary when trying to introduce new changes. The same is true when you are working with toddlers. With that in mind, you need to position their bed and other important stuff in their bedroom appropriately. As much as possible, position the new toddler bed at the same spot as their crib used to be.

Keep in mind that some toddlers get too stressed when they notice you moving everything related to them, so try to be consistent. You should also try to arrange and decorate their room similar to what they were used to. Observe your child's personality, as this will help you judge the best way to make the transition and position their stuff.

Empathize

One more thing you have to do as a parent is to empathize with your child. Take into account that every change is difficult. Even adults have a hard time accepting a sudden change, so expect your toddler to be stressed and pressured throughout the process. They may get too clingy, cry incessantly, or resist during the adjustment. You can handle that by showing empathy.

Let them know how much you understand how they feel and how difficult the transition is for them. You can also relay what you felt when you were their age and finally moved to a new bed. Your goal is to make them understand that someone understands their situation. Also, reassure them that you will always be around to guide them as they make the adjustments. That way, they will not feel too frightened of the new changes.

Dealing with Sudden Changes in a Preschooler's Sleep Schedule

Another major adjustment your child will have to go through is when they become of school age. They may feel extremely excited about this milestone, but it could also mean sudden changes in their sleep schedule that will greatly affect their lifestyle.

For instance, naptimes may get affected. Most kids around the ages of three to five require around eleven to thirteen hours of sleep each night. Also, most of these preschoolers have set naptimes during the day. These naps often range from one to two hours. You can expect these kids to stop napping upon reaching five.

You have to remember that each preschooler is different. While some stick to the nap routines they get used to, others refuse to nap once they become a preschooler. If your child is one who refuses a nap, you do not have to fret.

The technique here is to remain calm and consistent. Moreover, set a goal to make them get a minimum of eleven hours of sleep every night. That way, you do not have to worry too much if they ditch the nap during the daytime. Just make sure you also replace this ditched nap with quiet time or downtime involving relaxing activities, such as reading.

Another thing to keep in mind is that once your child gets into preschool, they may feel extremely tired once they come home. It is because of school activities and routines, especially if they have just started taking part in them. With that said, you should try to make adjustments to their routines, particularly those involving their sleep.

That way, they will restore lost energy and wake up feeling refreshed to take on the day. The following tips will make it easier for your child to adjust to their new life as a preschooler:

• *Set a regular bedtime* - Try to avoid putting them to bed too early, though. Your goal is to make them get into the habit of falling asleep thirty minutes after you put them to bed. Once they start preschool, you may want to schedule their bedtime a bit later so that they may achieve that. You can set it at 8:00 or 9:00 in the evening to make it a lot easier for them to settle down.

• *Establish limitations and boundaries during bedtime* - For instance, if you already told them you would read them only one story, make sure you follow through with that. Never give in; otherwise, you will have a harder time training them.

• *Set aside a relaxing and quiet time before their sleep schedule* - Your goal here is to help your child calm down and relax before bedtime. Try to set aside a quiet time with them that takes around thirty to 45 minutes. Activities you can incorporate here are storytelling, quiet play, coloring, jigsaw puzzles, dressing up for bed, turning off the light, and staying away from screens and TV an hour or so before bedtime.

• *Give rewards* - One of the most effective ways to reinforce a new habit and make your child adjust to new routines is to offer rewards. If they successfully stay in their bed and sleep on time, then you can reward them. This will motivate them to stick to the habits, promoting faster adjustments.

Sleep training can be extremely challenging, especially if your child needs to face a major change that will require them to make a sudden and huge adjustment to their usual routines. You can help them by letting them know you will always be there for them.

Remember that one of the secrets to managing any transition and a major change in your child's sleeping habits and routines is your patience. Be patient and prepare yourself for resistance on their part.

Handle your child calmly and constantly reassure them that you are still around, even if they are already in a new room and bed. Eventually, they will get used to the routines and make the necessary adjustments.

Conclusion

Now that you have finished reading this book, you are armed with all the information required for successful toddler sleep training. Use all the mentioned tips as your guide, and you will certainly eliminate most, if not all, of the problems that might stop your toddler from getting their much-needed rest.

You can tweak the tips a bit based on your unique situation and your child's distinctive personality and behaviors. Note that you cannot expect all children to be the same, so their responses may also be different. With that said, pick those tips, strategies, and tricks guaranteed to help your child finally have better quality and sound sleep.

Moreover, you will be thankful if you are successful with sleep training because it will also mean longer and better sleep for you and your family.

Here's another book by Meryl Kaufman that you might like

www.ingramcontent.com/pod-product-compliance
Lightning Source LLC
Chambersburg PA
CBHW050512240426
43673CB00004B/194